# OH GOD, OH GOD, OH GOD!

# OH GOD, OH GOD, OH GOD!

young adults speak out about
sexuality &
christian spirituality

Heather Godsey
Lara Blackwood Pickrel, eds.

CHALICE
PRESS

ST. LOUIS, MISSOURI

Bible quotations, unless otherwise noted, are from the *New Revised Standard Version Bible,* copyright 1989, Division of Christian Education of the National Council of the Churches of Christ in the United States of America. Used by permission. All rights reserved.

Scripture quotations marked (NIV) are taken from the HOLY BIBLE, NEW INTERNATIONAL VERSION®. NIV®. Copyright © 1973, 1978, 1984 by International Bible Society. Used by permission of Zondervan Publishing House. All rights reserved.

Cover and interior design: Elizabeth Wright

Visit www.chalicepress.com and check out the
WTF: Where's The Faith? page on Facebook.

10  9  8  7  6  5  4  3  2                    14  15  16  17  18  19


Print: 9780827227309    EPUB: 9780827227354    EPDF: 9780827227361


**Library of Congress Cataloging–in–Publication Data**

Oh, God, oh, God, OH, GOD! : young adults talk about sexuality and embodiment in Christian spirituality / edited by Lara Blackwood Pickrel and Heather Godsey.
    p. cm.
  ISBN 978-0-8272-2730-9
  1.  Sex—Religious aspects—Catholic Church. 2.  Human body—Religious aspects—Catholic Church. 3.  Young adults—Sexual behavior.  I. Pickrel, Lara Blackwood. II. Godsey, Heather. III. Title.


BX1795.S48O36 2010
241'.66—dc22

                                                  2009047416

# Contents

# OK, so here's the deal...

If you're like us, you've had plenty of "WTF?" moments with church and you asked one question.

No, not *that* one. OK, maybe *that* one. At first. But that quick, flip question led to another, more important question: ***Where's The Faith?***

Faith in a God who can be present in both scripture and science. Faith that allows us to meet our neighbors on equal ground, no matter their ethnic, religious, or economic background. Faith that folks in their teens, twenties, and thirties have something to contribute to the world, that they have big questions and big ideas about God, politics, sex, culture, the economy, justice, and what it means to be a human being.

We decided we wanted a series that brought as many young adult voices to the table as possible to talk in authentic, honest ways. These aren't slackers. They aren't overgrown adolescents. Instead of being talked about, or having questions posed about them, young adults are the ones framing the discussion, pushing the envelope, sharing their stories.

Discuss these stories amongst yourselves, or discuss them with us (series editors Brandon Gilvin and Christian Piatt) on Facebook on the WTF: Where's The Faith? page.

Read on.


Brandon and Christian

# Introduction

"Lions, and tigers, and bears! Oh my!
LIONS, AND TIGERS, AND BEARS! OH MY!"

Every time I reflect on the essays and topics that come together in this project, this familiar chant comes to mind. Within the context of this book, such a well-known proclamation of irrational fear could just as easily be replaced with statements like:

"We can't talk about sexuality in Sunday School. That would be inappropriate."

"The church shouldn't teach sexual education—I just wouldn't feel comfortable hearing my pastor talk about reproductive anatomy!"

"I don't know how I feel about our pastor's pregnancy. It is uncomfortable for me to hear her preach right now—in a way, it is too distracting."

When love, sexuality, and embodiment are brought up within the context of faith, the church, or spirituality, a corporate shudder travels throughout the body of Christ, and with that shudder comes confusion, resentment, and isolation. It is as though a large portion of ourselves must be left at the door as we enter into communities of faith.

Why can't Christians speak about real human experiences within the church? What causes us as a people of faith to believe that our hearts, sexualities, and bodies must be silenced and scrubbed before we enter the church or stand before God? Who says that a single minister of any age can't have a sexual relationship? What would happen if people of faith did discuss issues of sex and sexuality, the body, reproduction, and love relationships openly and without shame or fear? These are a few of the questions Heather and I had in mind as we began the task of recruiting contributors for this volume.

We sought to be both diverse and specific in our gathering of stories, hoping they would represent the gamut of gender, sexual, economic, ethnic, theological, and ideological diversity of the church, while also focusing on the unique needs, perspectives, and issues facing a new generation of ordained and lay church leaders. Above all else, we desired for this volume to provide young adults with both a resource of their own and an opportunity to share their prophetic voices, successful programs and projects, and innovative ideas in the areas of love, sex(uality), and embodiment.

This project is not perfect. Though our group of authors is diverse in many ways, some perspectives are glaringly absent or underrepresented. We have essays by college first-years and ordained ministers, single folk and married couples, parents, non-parents, and those who hope to be parents. Men and women are represented, voices speak out of varying regions and socioeconomic backgrounds, and different theological perspectives coexist in the pages that follow. But for various reasons (some beyond our control and some that I am certain were within our control), these voices are primarily from white heterosexual individuals. We deeply regret this fact and pray that as a response to this volume, young adult leaders and writers of all ethnic backgrounds will come forward to share their stories and deepen our reflection. We also fervently pray that one day it will become a less intimidating and dangerous task for ministers and laypeople of alternative sexual orientations to tell their truths and voice their experiences within the life of the church.

In the meantime, our hope is that this volume of truth telling will serve as a starting point for a larger conversation and a means by which new and authentic community begins to gel. Love, sex(uality), and embodiment are powerful realities. And though they often seem to get in the way of consensus or relationship, in truth they are a large portion of what unites us. Read. Think. Discuss. Let the conversation begin!

Lara Blackwood Pickrel
Heather Godsey
Coeditors

# The Silver Ring and the Ring of Fire

## When "True Love Waits" Meets Real Life

Chapter 1

*And he said, "Woe also to you lawyers! For you load people with burdens hard to bear, and you yourselves do not lift a finger to ease them."*
• Lk. 11:46

*For love is as strong as death,*
*Passion fierce as the grave.*
*Its flashes are flashes of fire,*
*A raging flame.* • Song 8:6

On a spring day in 1993 at a gathering of youth in Nashville, a new program called True Love Waits formed a new front in Baptist ministry: to get as many youth and young adults as possible to sign "commitment cards," pledging not to have sex until marriage. Within a few months, a group of Baptist youth presented 100,000 signed cards to the Southern Baptist convention in Houston. Within six months True Love Waits had its own hotline, newsletter, and staff. Within a few years the program spread to college campuses in the United States and to missions in Africa to combat HIV/AIDS. Hundreds of thousands of students and young people filled out commitment cards. According to True Love Waits' online FAQ, their theological grounding comes from God's "plan for marriage" in Genesis 2:24: "A man will leave his father and mother and be united to his wife, and they will become one flesh" (NIV). The admonitions in Hebrews 13:4 also help shape the plan: "Marriage should be honored by all, and the marriage bed kept pure, for God will judge the adulterer and all the sexually immoral" (NIV). Linking those verses to True Love Waits, the way that the FAQ writers have, seems to leave out some rhetorical steps: "The Bible speaks of sexual immorality, so there must also be such a thing as sexual morality, right? That morality is based on God's plan for sex."[1]

"God's plan for sex," as outlined in True Love Waits and other youth and young adult purity programs such as the Silver Ring Thing, is that human sexuality in any form should only occur in a marriage between a man and a woman.

True Love Waits advocates for waiting on more than just vaginal intercourse. As the FAQ explains: "Sexual purity means saying no to sexual intercourse, oral sex, and even sexual touching. It means saying no to a physical relationship that causes you to be 'turned on' sexually. It means not looking at pornography or pictures that feed sexual thoughts." Thus, any stimulating forms of physical touching or, with the inclusion of pornography, stimulating images are against God's comprehensive "plan." Anything that could cause the teenage mind to wander into sexual thoughts is a no-no in True Love Waits. The challenge, or impossibility if you want to call it that, is enormous when the goal for a teenager or young adult is to have no sexual thoughts whatsoever. How can hormone-driven young people learn to control millions of years of evolved sexuality? How can they totally ignore their sexuality until marriage and then somehow pull it out intact and ready for intimacy? What tools does True Love Waits offer to help young people overcome not only the pressure to have sex but also sexual thoughts?

My own experience with True Love Waits missed the devils in the details of those goals. Apparently when the rubber hits the road, purity seldom functions as its teachers and authors expect. My youth group went to Panama City Beach for our

True Love Waits retreat. At each teaching session we sat in nice carpeted conference rooms with sand on our feet and the salt dried on us from the ocean. They separated us by gender, so I was in the guy's session. About twenty of us, tired from body surfing and kicking sand everywhere, sat in a circle with a few dads, chaperones, and the senior pastor of our church. Concentration was minimal, as was motivation when the lesson was about not having or thinking about sex.

The retreat was pretty standard: We arrived Friday and played basketball for a while, had a worship session, ate some hamburgers for supper, and took a walk down to the beach. I gravitated toward a particular girl I liked, and we threw salt water back and forth on each other. We walked together and talked together but never about dating. Certainly, we never spoke about the subject of our retreat. I wanted to hold her hand or hug her. I had not yet heard from True Love Waits that such things were a risk to God's plan.

By Saturday morning all of our bunks were sandy, our things scattered across the dorms, and Linkin Park music blared from someone's portable speakers. We all screamed the lyrics, hanging out our doors and windows. Our youth director rented an inflatable boxing ring, and my best friend and I used it to beat the living hell out of each other. One older youth, whom I looked up to, played his guitar on a bench. I knew he had a past of marijuana and partying, things that I knew nothing about and that sounded terribly sinful to me. This also made his devotion all the more sincere. I watched him lose himself in his music. I envied him for it. Later when I talked to him he was accepting, although even at that age I knew my conversations were weird.

Other retreats with my youth group were about reconnecting with God, about learning that God loved and accepted us no matter who we were. Other retreats were about fellowship, whether through hanging out with the other guys or trying my best to hold a particular girl's hand during prayer time. They were times to forget trigonometry, *The Scarlet Letter*, and the smelly and awkward locker room. They were times when the youth group bonded despite their different cliques or their families' incomes.

But we knew from the beginning this retreat was going to be different.

Sex in our youth group was one of the three big sins, up there with drugs and drinking. They all sort of went together and seemed to lead to one another. Cussing was also big, but it was a lesser sin. Later I wondered why pride, greed, and prejudice took a backseat to Coors. Our youth director, thankfully, focused more on God's love than on sin in his messages, but when we did discuss sin, those three things received the most attention.

By Saturday afternoon we were in a circle writing anonymous questions about sex, purity, God, marriage, or anything else we could come up with. A few questions were legitimate: How far is too far? What if you really love someone? Other questions were more tangential: Is it okay to masturbate? Most, by far, were irrelevant, some of them not even questions: The ocean made my nipples hard.

These questions came after we were told the basics of True Love Waits: saving sex until marriage, God's "plan for marriage," and our call to be sexually pure. I regret that we couldn't come up with more nuanced questions about true love, the possibility of failed marriages, what made a marriage work, how to look for compatible girlfriends or boyfriends, to what degree emotional intimacy must be avoided before marriage, and so on. No, by and large we teenage boys, covered in sand and sweat, looked forward to lunch and getting back to the beach.

Saturday night was our come-to-Jesus worship service. For a little while, True Love Waits took a backseat to worship as the youth director and that older youth I looked up to played the songs that nourished me through high school. I sat next to the girl I liked. Sometimes I would look over to see if she had her eyes closed, her hands lifted. I was never sure which to do. My best friend was close by, and he too had his arms lifted. He always was less inhibited than I. Moments like those are my happiest memories from my youth group: worshiping with friends and people I looked up to and hearing those songs sung so sincerely. Outside I could hear the waves under the moonlight and their sound, their image, came together with the music. God was present there, in the assuring way that our young souls needed God to be.

Sunday morning we had another session. By this time everyone was sunburned, dirty, and tired. We worshiped, mostly the fast, happy songs of the contemporary repertoire. Then came the rings. The church paid for them, and we had all given our ring sizes beforehand. We signed our pledge cards without fanfare, almost like exchanging addresses from summer friends, and put on our rings. Then back in those cramped vans to listen to Third Day CDs until we got home.

The Monday at school after a retreat was always a tough time. On the way to school I thought about what I would say when people asked me about the ring. "I'm saving myself for marriage" sounded pretty weak coming from a sophomore geek in an oversized T-shirt.

High school went on. Youth group passed by in a flurry of ice cream socials and movie nights. I grew from the awkward sophomore to a more confident (but still awkward) senior and had others look up to me the same way I had looked up to the older youth in my time. Many of us kept our rings, but slowly they disappeared from the hands that went on that retreat. They were lost, some intentionally, others by accident, and others abandoned. My own ring came and went through a few relationships, and with it the guilt caused by knowing that I, in some cases, had gone against the commitment it symbolized. I knew that God would forgive me, but what damage had I done to myself or, as True Love Waits tends to focus on, my future spouse?

Then college happened. I graduated from high school and went to the University of Tennessee, a whole other school in a whole other state, where I and two others were the only people from Cordele, Georgia, among 30,000 college students. A family friend was excited about such a complete relocation, telling me that it was my chance to reinvent myself as whatever I wanted to be. The move was tough on my faith—leaving the youth group that nourished me and being on my own. On UT's campus a whole street is lined with student ministries: Roman Catholics, all the mainline Protestants, and even a few odd ones like Seventh-Day Adventists and Mormons tucked in along the side streets. My youth group was United Methodist, so I went there first, after my period of spiritual isolation.

How different the Wesley Foundation was from my youth group. I had grown up going to traditional services, but I spent much more time in contemporary services, usually in gyms or at outdoor concerts. At Wesley we met in a fifty-year-old chapel under a vaulted ceiling painted with Christian heraldry and Cherokee emblems of peace. Gold stars littered the eaves, and an iron cross hung over the altar, suspended as by air. Our hymns were without fail from the hymnal, and seeing college kids sing them willingly was a new thing for me. Each Wesley service had communion, something that was monthly at my old home church. No one lifted hands there; it was a different emotion of worship. Later I would find an Episcopalian "prayer for quiet confidence" that best described it.

The people were different as well. I was always shy, so for the first few Sundays I attended, I came and went without meeting many people. When I finally did connect, it was because I saw a briar pipe on the piano and asked whose it was. I met its owner along with his friends who lived at the Wesley Foundation. We talked about pipes, *Lord of the Rings*, and all the things I was interested in at the time. Awkward freshman that I was, they accepted me and welcomed me every time I came to Wesley. Not only that, I became their friend.

They were different from the people in my youth group. Rarely did we talk about God, Jesus, or any particular plan they had. These people drank, smoked, cussed, and told dirty jokes, all things I had tried hard to avoid during high school. At the same time, they attended every service, some even getting up early on Sunday to go down the street to another United Methodist Church (in addition to Wesley services in the evening). They talked to the homeless people around campus and gave them food from Wesley's kitchen. They welcomed everyone who came through those doors. I was confused at first, thinking about how people could do the things I knew of as wicked and still be in the church. The more I watched them, the more quiet goodness seemed present in their actions. It reminded me of the youth I looked up to several years before.

Coming to peace with their drinking and smoking, I began to change. Monday nights they had a "pipe and cigar club" where they sat around making a huge cloud of tobacco smoke and watching folks on the sidewalks. I bought a pipe and joined right in. One Sunday afternoon I found them drinking on the porch. It was Bud Lite from a cooler in plastic cups. I picked one up and had my first beer.

I agreed with them that the street preachers with signs saying "God hates Fags" were wrong, even though people at my home church had spoken of homosexuality as a sin.

I joined in singing those old hymns and grew a new appreciation for Charles Wesley.

I walked with them Sunday morning to that downtown church and lost myself in its choir and in the tall reaches of its Gothic nave.

I adapted. In adapting, I challenged my old notions that alcohol was evil, that homosexuals were against God's plan, and that outwardly emotional worship was a requirement of faith. In fact my idea of God's "plan" grew hazy as its shortsightedness became more and more apparent. I went from believing in a God who dwelt in single Bible verses and upraised hands to one who worked in quiet confidence, dwelt mysteriously in gatherings under vaulted stars and pipe smoke alike, who crafted from his people kindness through, rather than in spite of, their flaws. God became bigger, filling the places around me that I never knew God would be present in. As the burden of fighting against certain thoughts and behaviors decreased, the easy burden of living in grace gave me room to breathe.

*God became bigger*

This adaptation came partly from a new environment and good teaching. It came more than anything from a new fellowship. Not that my old youth friends were bad; in fact, we still support each other in our faith. But they, like me, have grown and found news ways of faith. As Christ makes all things new, so my youth group faith was eclipsed by a newer, more open faith. I much preferred the plan of God's mysterious moving in fellowship and worship to any that a few Web site FAQ writers have thrown together from solitary Bible verses.

All of these changes make the backdrop for the change in my sexual understanding. I have mentioned how my college friends drank, cussed, and so on, and nonetheless led lives of grace-filled acceptance. About two years into college, a year after I saw that pipe laying on the piano, I was sitting out on the porch with the pipe's owner when his girlfriend stopped by. I didn't know he was seeing anyone up until that point. I soon saw much more of her as she came to Wesley events, welcoming people just as the rest of the group did and acting in the same kindness I admired in them.

She also spent the night with him nearly every weekend. He was handsome, and she was pretty. It was obvious, even to an awkward sophomore, what was going on. They had been dating for some time before I met her. Today they are still together, and their relationship has been a committed one.

By this time I was okay with drinking (we were having "Thirsty Thursdays" weekly) and cussing and all that, but sex was different. It went beyond one person and inculpated two, and seemed just plain sketchy. Feelings of guilt and confusion followed my thoughts about sex. When my friends entered into the picture, I didn't know how to reconcile a committed unmarried couple fully engaged in their relationship, who also clearly bore the fruits of the spirit. That silver ring I had since stopped wearing declared that those two things could not go together.

Freud said that anyone with a healthy sexual life would be free from neuroses. In my experience, he is right. After taking college psychology and biology classes, it made sense that, as human animals, we have our procreative instincts, and they aren't going anywhere anytime soon. Sex is hardwired into our system. Despite what True Love Waits says, I believe people don't get away from sexual drives except in a healthy sexual relationship between two committed partners or through serious asceticism. The desert monastics fought sexual fantasies all the time, and all they had to look at was the Sahara. Sex is biologically unavoidable, so how can Christians live a life of total, even mental, chastity without rigorous spiritual tools?

In a scene in Nella Larsen's novel *Quicksand,* the protagonist, who has missed relationship after relationship and hasn't been able to consummate anything throughout the book, goes to an energetic worship service and has a religious experience best described as an orgasm. At least that is the point of it in the book: All her pent-up sexual energy is released through passionate worship. I've seen a similar thing happen in Saturday night worship at large retreats. My point is that because sex is unavoidable, its energies will find their ways into other areas if the normal channels aren't open. They might escape into worship, music, sports, video games, or just about anything else. Our human desire for intimacy and the release of sexual energies will find its way out if sex, its normal release valve, is unavailable. So if someone follows the traditional Christian ethic of chastity, they had better be aware of the passions that will result and be ready to deal with them. Such is the challenge of saving sex until marriage, and they didn't say a thing about it in True Love Waits. A $24.95 silver ring cannot contain attraction, desire, and the need for intimacy or passion.

> Our human desire for intimacy and the release of sexual energies will find its way out if sex is unavailable.

If I could go back to that sandy retreat center room today, I have many more questions I would write and hand in: How can I satisfy my need for intimacy until I get married? It's going to be a few years until I can realistically support a family and get married, yet I'm in a committed relationship headed that way, so what are the real dangers of fully practicing our relationship? Are there dangers? Why does the United Methodist Book of Discipline, in 2008, still prohibit homosexuality even after most scientists affirm it is biological, a part of DNA? Should I even tell my partner I love her, or does that impinge upon the intimacy reserved for marriage?

How far is too far? A kiss, a hug, getting her roses on Valentine's day?

What if I really love someone, and it's going to be years before we can get married?

Unfortunately, we tend to face these questions without the wisdom of our families, our churches, or our particular saints. The rules are set and unyielding to inquiry. For me, the plan outlined on a Web site, summarized on a card that came with

The Silver Ring and the Ring of Fire

a ring, was insufficient in equipping my mind and heart for the challenges True Love Waits, and indeed life, presented to me. Love is a burning thing; the silver ring is ill-equipped to overcome the ring of fire.

### Additional Resources

Arterburn, Stephen, Fred Stoeker, and Mike Yorkey. *Every Young Man's Battle: Strategies for Victory in the Real World of Sexual Temptation.* Colorado Springs: Waterbrook Press, 2002.

Arterburn, Stephen, Shannon Ethridge, and Josh McDowell. *Every Young Woman's Battle: Guarding Your Mind, Heart, and Body in a Sex-Saturated World.* Colorado Springs: Waterbrook Press, 2004.

Harris, Joshua. *I Kissed Dating Goodbye.* Sisters, Oreg.: Multnomah Press, 1997.

LifeWay Student Ministry: True Love Waits. www.lifeway.com/tlw

Winner, Lauren. *Real Sex: The Naked Truth about Chastity.* Grand Rapids: Brazos Press, 2006.

# Questions \ for Discussion and Contemplation

1 What were your earliest introductions to sexual morality? Did the church or anyone of faith provide guidance or advice? How did it impact your later experiences?

2 What was your experience of faith like in high school and how did that change during college?

3 This author finds fellowship in a campus ministry. Did you participate in a campus ministry of some kind? What sorts of experiences did you have, and how do those shape your faith now?

4 True Love Waits offers a sexual ethic exclusive to heterosexual marriage. As teens and young adults become aware of their sexuality at earlier ages, how can the church help homosexual young adults reconcile their sexual orientation with their identities as children of God?

# Hookup Jesus

## Spirituality and Collegiate Sexuality

**Chapter 2**

As the morning light streamed through the window, I opened my eyes and realized the wall was the wrong color. Crap! I'd done it again. I'd been so good for so long. Here I was a junior, supposedly way past this stage, the stage where the walls and the bed were not mine. Bits and pieces floated past me—vodka and O.J., somebody's birthday party maybe? Colored pulsing lights, lots of room to dance, and him. Oh yeah—that's who was breathing next to me, lying there so I would have to crawl over him to get out. Him of the beautiful eyelashes and crooked grin. Him whose name everyone knew. The kind of him who would never have looked twice at my glasses-and-braces-wearing self in high school; the kind of him I would have swooned over from afar. Only this morning, I was in his room, in his bed. I allowed myself a moment to hug that fact, to feel triumphant and beautiful. And then I remembered. I remembered that this would get out, that the reputation I'd been assigned my freshman year still lingered. The reputation I didn't then, and still don't now, understand. I thought everyone did this—wasn't that all everyone talked about on Sunday evening in the cafeteria? How much they drank and who they mashed?

"Mash" was the term of the moment and almost ten years later, my students and my reading inform me that today the phrase is "hooking up"—a construction meant to convey a casual sexual encounter between two people, college-student-type people, who meet at a party or in a bar and proceed to spend the night together indulging in sexual acts ranging from kissing and heavy petting to oral sex to actual, honest-to-goodness intercourse. Of course, copious amounts of alcohol typically prime the pump, so to speak. Characteristically, neither person is looking, or will admit to looking, for a relationship. Rather, both acknowledge this as a one-time experience entered into because it feels good and because you're both pretty drunk. Sometimes a single mash becomes serial, something the two people do several times over the course of a few weeks; again never intending to enter into any sort of actual romantic relationship, mostly never having any real conversation. We called this "shacking."

**H**ooking up often involves lots of alchohol.

Mashing or shacking, nothing changes the fact that the one who falls asleep afterward in a strange bed will be doing the walk of shame through the parking lot the next morning. You find yourself praying no one notices; that those few hardy souls heading toward breakfast in the cafeteria will, out of courtesy, pretend not to see you.

I sighed deeply, realizing that it was after 9 a.m. on a Saturday, and someone was going to see me heading back. Fudge. I crawled over him, gathering my clothes, dressing quickly, grabbing my backpack which still held two empty alcohol bottles. They clinked and his eyes opened. "Hey, where you going?" he mumbled. "Gotta study," I replied, swinging the pack over my shoulder. "Here?" He was half-asleep and pretty confused. I just smiled and left.

According to the onslaught of articles and sociological studies in the last few years, hooking up has become a nationwide college campus phenomenon. Though the definition is vague, writers of all stripes, journalists and scholars alike, attempt to find answers to the following questions: Why are students engaging in this sort of behavior? What kinds of consequences result? And what can administrators and parents to do to alleviate the detrimental side effects?

Tellingly, the same themes emerge over and over again. Hookup culture appears on campus because college is historically a liminal place where students experiment with different ways of living. Moreover, proximity to one another and an environment that encourages a cult of achievement provides both opportunity and justification. Intentionally vague, the term *hooking up* serves both sexes' purposes in specific ways. As noted by Laura Sessions Stepp in her volume *Unhooked,*[1] the spectrum of meanings hooking up encompasses allows women to engage in casual sexual relationships while also protecting their reputations. Because no one knows the exact nature of her experience, she can claim it to be as innocuous as possible or leave everyone wondering. By turns, Michael Kimmel, author of *Guyland,*[2] asserts that the inherent vagueness allows men to encourage their peers to assume far more than perhaps occurred. In this way, both sexes assure themselves of the continued approval of their peers, while still embracing casual sexual experiences of a sort.

In a postfeminist world, Stepp observes that girls raised in a culture of no-holds-barred achievement understand the message of success as saving force only too well. They compete not only on the playing field against each other, but in the classroom against the boys for the best grades. There's no end to success, they're told. They can do anything they want, succeed at anything they want. In fact, they should.[3] The cult of success impresses upon young women the necessity of high achievement, a necessity that has them spending every second of their young lives studying to get the A, networking for the perfect internship, creating the perfect body, and building the perfect resume. All of it done in the name of snagging the perfect, lucrative job. With so many other commitments, who has the time to devote to building a relationship? Besides, everyone wants to get established and succeed in their careers before settling down into a committed relationship. Even parents insist that young women will have plenty of time for relationship building later. For now, hooking up solves all kinds of dilemmas.

Kimmel agrees. Many of his interviewees point to their overloaded schedules as reason number one to avoid any sort of romantic entanglement, while others simply don't see the point of choosing one woman when they can hook up with a different one every weekend. As well, the fact remains that on most campuses the party scene and its attendant hookups is, or at least appears to be, the only social scene available. Those who don't participate, the story goes, can likely count on spending the evenings doing homework in their dorm rooms.

Beyond the culture of achievement, both Stepp and Kimmel posit that the college environment where everyone has easy access to one another contributes to hookup culture. While Stepp points to "coed dorms and unrestricted visitation hours"[4] as factors enabling hookup culture at the large universities she visited, the culture of my own small liberal arts college was vastly different and yet still fostered the hookup mentality. Hovering around one thousand, my college's enrollment as well as its elite regional reputation provided students with a sense of entitlement and pride. When multiplied by the predominance and centrality of Greek organizations to all aspects of campus life, the campus culture was ripe for precisely the type of hookup behavior both authors chronicle.

Not only were we pressed to succeed, to fill every minute of our days with worthy endeavors, much as Stepp and Kimmel describe, but in such a small community you come to know each other, even if only by sight. Indeed, because I knew who belonged on campus and who did not, I often felt more secure visiting and attending parties in the men's dorms than I might have at a bigger university.[5] I didn't fear accepting drinks from fraternity men because I had classes with them, ate with them, and believed they would never try to harm me or ask more than I was willing to give. Because I had at least a passing familiarity with these men, I felt it was a safe place to abandon my inhibitions and drink as much as I pleased. Of course, feeling both safe and often very drunk, I felt emboldened to act on impulses as they occurred to me. And my dorm room or theirs was, luckily, close at hand.

As Stepp notes, a natural extension of the "you go, girl" feminism that makes women want to achieve is an attempt to claim one's own sexuality in the exact ways young men do—by using it. Never afraid to call myself a feminist, I too fell into the trap of assuming that engaging in sexual acts while attempting to turn off my emotions was my feminist birthright. Not only could I attract and repel men at will, but I could use them for my own pleasure, just as any man might use a woman. I wasn't a slut; I was a strong young woman owning her sexuality.

Own it I did late into my first year at an alcohol-soaked party where I finally bit off more than I could chew. A prospective student visiting for the weekend had beautiful ice-blue eyes, and the more I drank the prettier they got. I believe I simply walked right up to him in the middle of the hallway and began kissing him without so much as introducing myself. Although his host had confiscated his khakis and shoes to prevent him from leaving, the two of us skittered down the stairs, across the parking lot, and up to my room anyway. An hour later, loud knocks and stage whispers demanded the boy's return. And this is where I discover something both Kimmel and Stepp bring to light: While hooking up may seem the only social scene in town, doing so too often or too visibly leads to adverse consequences.

*Is hooking up the only scene?*

Not only is one at risk for STDs, but sexual assault remains prevalent on college campuses. Several of Kimmel's interviewees, both male and female describe situations that can only be interpreted as assault or even rape. Under strict scrutiny, I can't claim to have experienced assault, but I imagine that it was only because I was lucky. Instead, I experienced a gradual deadening of the soul, the realization that all this hooking up that was supposed to be fun and empowering actually left me feeling empty and depressed. Not to mention without the male companionship I imagined it netting me. After the incident with the prospective student, one fraternity member hissed at me, "Your name is mud with us!" And while he held little influence and really spoke only for himself, I began to notice that what I had previously thought was friendship and inclusion was now more of a tolerant amusement. I had become a hanger-on, a groupie.

As my sophomore year rolled on, I found myself choosing to write papers on Friday nights rather than venture across the parking lot. Withdrawing into my major, I clung to my course load and my job as a writing tutor and professor's assistant. I no longer felt beautiful or strong or sexual, spending most days in an oversized pair of purple corduroy overalls or jeans and a large fleece sweatshirt. Cognizant now that many girls had been criticizing me for my previous behavior, I longed to disappear into the woodwork, to forget that I had once thought it was okay to be sexually active because so many others were. I also wanted to forget that, while I had tried to pretend that it didn't matter when my latest hookup barely acknowledged me on campus, I longed to be loved, to be chosen, and had seen no other way of inviting a young man to do so.

This is yet another consequence Kimmel and Stepp highlight. Though both young men and women profess to not be interested in a relationship, though they claim to not have time to commit, they do want to be married someday and secretly yearn for intimacy. Women especially seek this, but because dating has gone the way of the dinosaurs, they participate in the hookup culture hoping that a hookup will lead to a relationship. When it doesn't, they find themselves feeling oddly unsettled, disappointed, and perhaps even a bit hurt. These feelings can snowball over time, leading to depression and a sense of emptiness that students don't always have the vocabulary to describe.

Donna Freitas takes on this disappointment when she steps into the discussion with her book, *Sex and the Soul*.[6] Interviewing students at seven different institutions about both their religious/spiritual commitments and their sex lives, she finds few students who manage to successfully integrate their sexual activity with their religious upbringing or commitments. Without any guidance from older adults, the students in Freitas' survey find themselves either entrenched in a rigid purity culture that prohibits acknowledging sexuality and denies grace, or in a spiritual-but-not-religious realm that brackets sexuality, effectively separating it from any spiritual meaning or religious commitments.

Though she includes evangelical colleges in her study, she finds that the large public universities, the private nonsectarian colleges, and the catholic colleges incubate hookup culture. These institutions are populated with students who claim the spiritual-but-not-religious moniker, who manage to divorce their sexual behavior from whatever religious or spiritual beliefs their parents may have instilled. In this way, students who were raised in a church or with a religious background compartmentalize religion or even jettison it wholesale. In fact, as Freitas points out, most students are used to keeping their religion private in their campus communities and their sex private in their religious ones.[7] So compartmentalization continues, and no one thinks anything about it. But such separation does have consequences.

Portraying hookup culture as a "social hazing process,"[8] Freitas finds that 41 percent of her survey respondents articulated some form of regret for their actions. She calls this the "dashed hopes" hookup.[9] In fact, her results show that hookups are not as prevalent as they seem. Rather, what she refers to as a "powerful peer minority"[10] actually promotes the perception that social life really does revolve around alcohol and having sex. "The hookup culture, though pervasive," she claims, "does not actually appeal to the average student."[11]

So I spent my first two years of college participating in a social rite that only seemed widespread. Most likely it appeared that way because of the incredible power Greek social groups had over those living on campus. Without a car and desperate to be liked, to produced evidence that I was not the ugly, socially inept person I felt lurking underneath, I bought into the Greek version of the social scene unquestioningly. Though I couldn't afford to join a sorority, I sought validation by attempting to ingratiate myself with fraternity men. Hooking up seemed the easiest way of doing so.

Like many of the students at Freitas' spiritual-but-not-religious colleges, I grew up with a strong church background. In fact, the college itself was affiliated with the mainline denomination of the congregation I attended. I had years of Sunday school and church camp behind me, as well as the love of a congregation who thought I hung the moon. Unfortunately, none of them ever had a thing to say about sexuality.

Hookup Jesus

The campus ministry I sporadically attended was similarly closemouthed, and I often felt judged by its members. So I too carefully divorced my religious worldview from my social activities until my depression and alienation moved me to the brink of agoraphobia by my senior year. Left with no earthly idea how to put those two parts of myself together, not until I began doing field education my second year in seminary did I finally seek out counseling and begin to heal by carefully constructing a bridge between my sexual self and my religious study.

With the help of a good counselor, I began to articulate my intense longing for emotional and physical intimacy. I yearned to feel connected to another person, to be known thoroughly and loved unconditionally. I didn't simply crave the sexual relationship, I wanted the existential affirmation I felt when touched. To experience physical intimacy was to prove that I did, in fact, exist, that I wasn't invisible or imaginary. Hooking up was the way in which I sought to establish my own humanity.

As I waded deeper in to the worlds of feminist theologies, I could easily see that I was experiencing the fundamental crux of the Divine-human relationship. Something about human-to-human intimacy called forth the Divine and created space for the sacred. Seeking physical intimacy, I began to see, was an allegory for seeking God. The mythology of the Genesis Garden story communicates to us our connectedness to God and to each other. Adam and Eve are naked and unashamed before each other and before God. Only the fruit of the knowledge of good and evil brings the shame and disconnection that places them at a remove from God and each other. Feeling always this disconnection, we seek that which might restore us to ourselves and to God. Hooking up was simply a new way of enacting the age old tale.

The way back to intimacy and connection seemed to hinge upon the notion of *imago Dei*, or "the image of God." Genesis 1 reminds us that our whole selves both physical and spiritual were created in the image of God and that we are indeed good. My cravings for physical intimacy weren't merely allegorical;

they were real, and they were part of the total package God fashioned and endorsed. I am, I realized, body and soul, a piece of God's will, a reflection of the divine imagination. Moreover, so is everyone else. Hooking up had created such dissonance because in seeking my own humanity, I had failed to see the humanity of my partner. I went looking for connection but had not done so in a way that allowed the other person his own reality. So rather than bringing me closer to others, hooking up had driven me even further away. And the further I moved from human connection, the further I moved from God.

Given this, I should not have been surprised to find myself hiding in clothes three sizes too big and shunning the large communal tables in the cafeteria. I was lost, alone in a world void of coherence and lacking any framework for interpretation. My body was alien to me, and God was nowhere to be found. Even as I prepared for seminary with courses in world religions and early Christianity, I found myself numb to any applicable personal meaning. God was an academic concept, religion an area of scholarship. Neither impacted me on a spiritual level. I couldn't pray, and I didn't worship. Even my Sunday job as a children's minister in a small church wasn't immune. Though I loved the church and those children, I felt it was a sort of sociological experiment, an exercise in the art of Christian education—not a ministry and certainly not a call from God. At school, my study of literature became a study of American sexuality in all its forms. I wrote papers on the use of sexual euphemisms and crude language. I studied how characters related to each other, how gender and sexuality could be used to interpret a particular novel or identify the motivation of a certain character. Nothing was sacred, and everything was profane. My advisor, an edgy fashionista from California fascinated by pop culture and well-schooled in gender studies, was delighted. She had no way of knowing from where my interest sprang, and I lacked the words, not to mention the self-knowledge, to tell her. I entered seminary sad and lonely, trying desperately not to cry anytime anyone was kind or made a gesture toward friendship. That I would eventually be unable to hold the sadness or tolerate the alienation was a given. Thus my entry into the world of the counseling center, a sojourn almost every candidate for ministry should, and does, make for him or herself at some point in the journey toward God.

Struggling as I was to make sense of myself, I also struggled to make sense of Jesus. Inherently suspicious of the "Jesus died for our sins" Christology, I searched for alternative ways of articulating Jesus' purpose. Courses in faith and pop culture, and American religious history provided an ever-widening sense that we often created Jesus in our image and for our own purposes. So I'm not surprised that listening to the illustrious Amy-Jill Levine present a very human, very Jewish Jesus gave rise to my preference for following this human Jesus over worshiping the Divine Christ. I could see in him the same urge to connect with people, to witness to the presence of God by being present for the least of these or really for any of these. In her seminar on ecological theology, Sallie McFague called this the loving eye—the act of looking at the other and recognizing God's presence calling for compassion. I don't know if Jesus was married or slept with Mary Magdalene or ever had an "impure" thought. However, I do know that this man was called to extend grace to others, to see God's light burning within them and to affirm it as good. Ultimately I began to see myself as good too. It turns out that Jesus didn't die for my sins, but instead he died as a witness to the power of the world to ignore God's presence in the other. Jesus died because of the one sin that leads to so many others—inhumanity.

> **J**esus died as a witness to the power of the world to ignore God's presence in the other.

Donna Frietas points out that many students find themselves in my situation with few resources upon which to draw. She not only offers sample questions one might ask of college administrations about sex and spirituality on campus, but emphatically calls for "Parents and colleges...to empower students to challenge that powerful minority which controls the peer sex ethic by emphasizing that they are not only not alone, they have strength in numbers."[12] She extends this call to clergy as well, outlining a number of issues that need to be addressed from within a faith tradition. From my own experience, both as a student and as a campus minister, I see three theological anchor points from which to begin building a Christian collegiate sexual ethic that can successfully repudiate hookup culture without forcing students into an untenable purity paradigm: (1) that every body is created in the image of God and called good, (2) that human sexuality is a part of that created goodness, and (3) that Jesus lived and died as a fully incarnated body with all the attendant feelings and urges.

Finally, ten years later I am still recovering, still trying to process those undergraduate years, still yearning for intimacy and not always reaching for it in healthy ways. (Can you say brownies make you feel better?) But I have hope in the resurrection, in God's ability to make all things new.

## Additional Resources

Bell, Rob. *Sex God: Exploring the Endless Connections between Sexuality and Spirituality.* Grand Rapids: Zondervan, 2007.

Freitas, Donna. *Sex and the Soul: Juggling Sexuality, Spirituality, Romance, and Religion on America's College Campuses.* New York: Oxford, 2008.

Kimmel, Michael. *Guyland: The Perilous World Where Boys Become Men.* New York: HarperCollins, 2008.

Stepp, Laura Sessions. *Unhooked: How Young Women Pursue Sex, Delay Love, and Lose at Both.* New York: Riverhead Books, 2007.

# Questions for Discussion and Contemplation

1 In a church culture that seems to promote the compartmentalization of faith and sexuality, what is gained and what is lost? Is the reward of outward decency and simplicity worth the risk of alienation many people experience as a result of this compartmentalization?

2 In your experience, is it true that alienation from self, others, and God are intimately related? By failing to recognize the divinity in others, do we really begin to divorce ourselves from love of self and love of God?

3 Have you ever retreated into a more cerebral version of faith in order to manage and control the complexity of lived experience? Likewise, have you ever given all of your attention to strictly experiential faith in order to manage and control the complexity of God's mystery? What would it take to balance faith and reason?

4 What have we to gain from considering that Jesus might not have simply died for our sins but as a witness to the power of the world to ignore God's presence in the other?

5 What kinds of things would you include in a new sexual ethic for the church, one that both embraces the gift of sexuality and promotes seeking the image of God in our partners?

# Sexuality Education in the Church

## The "Eighters'" Method

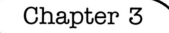

Chapter 3

My favorite camp game takes place at a very specific summer camp. It goes something like this: One boy in the center of the pool closes his eyes while a dozen or so others scatter around the shallow end. "Penis!" he shouts loudly. "Vagina!" they scream back in Marco-Polo fashion.

Ladies and gentlemen, welcome to Eighters' Camp.

### The Eighters' Model

In 1983, Trinity Presbyterian Church of Midland, Texas, approached Linda Goddard and asked her to create a biblically based sex education class. As word spread and this congregation's program grew, members of Memorial Christian Church in Midland began to discuss other ways they could use the curriculum. Ultimately, from her previous curriculum, Linda developed "Created to Be Me," a camp curriculum for graduated eighth graders that focuses on spirituality and sexuality. In the summer of 1987, the first Eighters' Camp opened at Lake Brownwood Christian Retreat; in the past twenty years it has spread to more than nine states and has touched the lives of more than 4,000 campers (and scores of counselors and parents).

Eighters' Camp isn't like other sex education programs out there. To begin with, God is involved and remains front and center throughout the whole process. While leaders give campers all the facts, details, and options on subjects ranging from contraception to the physical makeup of the body, every bit of information is placed in the context of the amazing plan that God has for each and every one of them. Kids at Eighters' Camp are never asked to wear a ring or publically declare their virginity until marriage because the program is not about guilting the campers into making a promise. Instead, leaders of the Eighters' program believe a decision to abstain from sex outside of marriage is a sacred promise between that individual, God, and his or her future spouse.

T he program is not about guilting the campers into making a promise.

Perhaps the most amazing thing about the Eighters' curriculum is the way it seamlessly weaves together spirituality and sexuality—two things that are not usually paired together. Human sexuality is not presented as something hidden or dirty. Instead, it is depicted as a beautiful gift given to us by God that, when used the way God intended, can have amazing results. Conversely, when it is misused, there are consequences for every action as well as forgiveness for mistakes.

During keynotes and small groups, soon-to-be ninth grade youth get to see and hear what the Bible says about sex and relationships. Morning keynotes are focused on biblical stories that deal with these two topics—these sessions vividly portray Adam and Eve's first moments together in the garden of Eden, the humanity of Jesus, and events such as Jesus' treatment of women and his incredible love for the outcast and lonely. Even Jesus' adolescence is discussed, which helps youth to see that Jesus does understand what being a teenager feels like.

In afternoon workshops, campers get a full education on dating, being sexually active, conception, contraceptives, and STIs.[1] Keynoters, counselors, and campers discuss the potential dangers of one-on-one dating before sixteen and dating pitfalls like the combination of dating and alcohol. Emphasis is placed on the powerful emotions experienced in sexual relationships, and the keynoters share personal stories illustrating the consequences of their own choices, not only to themselves, but to their future spouse. While abstinence is discussed and encouraged above all other options, the program educates youth about everything involving their sexuality. The guiding principle for this education is that as youth learn about human sexuality, they deserve truth and fact instead of myth and fear.

In small groups, youth discuss dating strategies including group dating and how to concentrate on being friends with someone prior to dating. Through workbook exercises, activities, and conversations, youth learn ways to keep God in the center of a relationship and how to spot a healthy relationship. On the flip side, youth also learn about the warning signs of an abusive relationship and discuss ways to get out before a relationship becomes truly dangerous.

Every evening culminates in worship, and youth participate fully in the worship services. They retell the stories they have learned each day and reflect on each day's lesson. Because of the active role the campers play in each worship experience, they are incredibly poignant, touching, and memorable—past campers often look back years later and remember the theme and message of each worship service that took place during their week.

The lessons learned in that week are irreplaceable. Each camper is loved and treated equally, no matter their age, history, or past choices. Eighters' stresses that you can have a fresh start with your spirituality and your sexuality, no matter what you have done in the past. God is waiting to help—all you have to do is ask.

### One Camper's Experience

My first experience with Eighters' Camp as a camper was in 1995. I remember vividly showing up at Lake Brownwood Christian Retreat (outside Brownwood, Texas) that day. Eighters' Camp (or "Sex Camp" as it was more commonly called) was legendary. I had heard about it for as long as I could remember. Older kids in my church came home gushing about it but would only reveal limited details. The camping program had originated in the Central Area, and for those of us in the Area's camping program, Eighters' was considered a rite of passage.[2]

I was a typical fourteen-year-old girl. I had a few close girlfriends at camp, but I was never really boy crazy. I was eager for Eighters' Camp and couldn't wait to see what it was all about. Nothing could have prepared me for what I was about to experience.

The week seemed to pass in a flash, and the information I learned was life changing. I had always thought of myself as a smart, talented girl, but I had never thought of myself as pretty. In my mind, beauty had to do with the women I saw in magazines or walking the runway, so I didn't think of my physical body as attractive. I was starving for someone besides my mother to think I was pretty. That week taught me that what I thought was beautiful was misconstrued. Through the curriculum and atmosphere of Eighters' Camp, I learned that I am indeed beautiful.

I had been raised to think that women were capable of anything, and Linda (who keynoted camp that week) showed me that I could not be held back because I was a woman. Through the keynotes, I found biblical confirmation that I was made worthy by God and in Christ I could achieve anything.

**A Camper Returns**

I took what I experienced that week with me throughout the next decade: the friends I had made, the information I had obtained, and the gift that awaited me if I could wait for it. During the next four years of high school I continued to attend CYF[3] events and even served on the Central Area's youth leadership council. I spent high school concentrating on friends, camp, and school, so upon graduating high school in 1999, I hadn't ever had a "real" romantic relationship. Two months later, I met Karl. We began dating and were married in the summer of 2001.

In the fall of 2003, I volunteered to be the youth director at my home church, First Christian Church in Iowa Park, Texas. The following spring, I took a job as the director of youth ministries at First Christian Church in Wichita Falls,

Texas. At this point I found Eighters' again. The director of our area's camp was Montie "Momma" Carroll. She had been a constant presence throughout my past camping experiences, and when she asked me to counsel Eighters' Camp that year, I immediately agreed.

It was the summer of 2005—ten years since my own Eighters' Camp. When I walked into the assembly hall, I immediately recognized Linda, and to my surprise, she recognized me.

"You were one of my campers," she said. "The singer."

I had been known for two things as a camper: I was dramatic, and I could sing. I was shocked that Linda could remember that far back to that short, awkward girl I had tried so hard to leave in the past.

That first year as an Eighters' counselor was an emotional roller coaster. I reexperienced the Eighters' curriculum and did quite a bit of soul searching. I realized how much had changed (I was an "adult," and I was married) and how much had remained the same (I still felt as strongly as ever that the Eighters' camping program was the single most important camp that a young person could ever experience).

The keynotes that year took on a new meaning for me, and the workshops were wonderfully embarrassing. I love to sit in the back of the room when the male anatomy is flashed onto the screen and watch all the heads in the room slowly slide down in their chairs as the giggling begins! I never get tired of watching *Am I Normal?*—a truly legendary sex-education video from the 1970s. (Linda tried to remove it from the curriculum a few years ago, and because of word of mouth and overwhelming demand, she brought it back.) I love when the female keynoter[4] discusses the first sexual encounter of Adam and Eve. But one story will always be my favorite.

The story of the bleeding woman brings me to tears every year. No one can tell that story like Linda. In her telling of the story, when Jesus touched that hemorrhaging women, he forever showed that women were not dirty or of less value than men because of their menstrual cycles—a stigma that exists to this day. Christ showed us through his compassion that we are all created equal and that the hemorrhaging woman's female anatomy was merely what made her woman, not something that condemned her. After all, God made her too.

The first worship of each Eighters' Camp holds a special place in my heart. Mary, the mother of Christ, has a monologue and then sings "Breath of Heaven." My first year, I was cast to play Mary, and Montie insisted that I sing the song. That first year I sang it for Linda, and the second year I sang it seven-months pregnant with my son. I've sung every year since.

Experiencing Eighters' again as an adult is such an amazing experience. I am probably one of the few who have been at Eighters' camp on both sides of adolescence. Watching youth gain the knowledge to help them navigate puberty, make educated decisions, and take hold of and own their sexuality without shame is by far one of the most satisfying experiences I have ever had.

### An Adulthood Affected

As it turns out, Eighters' Camp had yet another meaning waiting to reveal itself to me. In 2006, while pregnant with my son, Michael, I gained more than the average amount of weight. After a difficult labor, I was left with a beautiful baby boy, significant postpartum injuries, and an extra twenty-five pounds of weight.

For several months I was unable to stand for more than fifteen minutes without intense pain. Therefore, working out to lose the weight was simply out of the question. I began to hate being female. While I never harbored any resentment toward my son, I was filled with a smoldering anger for my physical femininity and the weight that I could do nothing about. I sunk into a depression I never told anyone about. Though it was obvious to my husband, I painted on a happy face to others around me.

In February of 2007, after much physical therapy, I slowly became able to walk comfortably and exercise. I looked at myself everyday in the mirror and hated what I saw. My 5'3" frame held 145 pounds and staring back at me out of the mirror was the most hideous thing I had ever seen. My old mind-set had taken hold: I was nothing if I was not physically beautiful.

My husband constantly told me how pretty I was, but nothing registered with me. I thought to myself, "Of course, he has to say I am beautiful. I am the mother of his child and his wife!"

I began to diet and work out feverishly. When my labor injuries ached, I pushed myself until I almost could not stand, and I deprived myself of food in order to lose more weight. One day as I scrolled though pictures on my computer, I found pictures of the previous year's Eighters' Camp. In the pictures, I was seven months pregnant, and I had never looked happier. A wave of emotion swept over me, and suddenly I remembered the central message of the Eighters' keynotes: I am "fearfully and wonderfully made!" In that moment I was filled with a new empowerment—once again I was so passionately proud to be a woman.

In the following months I altered my patterns. I continued to lose weight, but my mind-set had changed. When my body hurt, I listened to it. I didn't skip meals but began a healthy diet that helped me reach my goals. By the time Eighters' Camp rolled around again, I weighed 119 pounds, and I have continued to maintain that weight.

*I am fearfully and wonderfully made!!*

I still struggle with my physical appearance and have to remind myself continually that the size, shape, or look of my body does not determine my worth. It is a constant struggle for me, and if I had not had the experience of Eighters' to remind me of these truths, I'm not sure I would be the healthy, happy person I am now.

So as long as I am able, I will serve at Eighters' Camp, and as long as I have breath in my body, I will sing the praises of this amazing program—a gift to the church that has touched the lives of over 4,000 people. I will do so because Eighters' not only changed my life—it saved it.

### Additional Resources

Bell, Rob. *Sex God: Exploring the Endless Connections between Sexuality and Spirituality.* Grand Rapids: Zondervan, 2007.
CLER Ministries. www.clerministries.org. At this Web site you can find information about the Eighters' Camp programs,

as well as information on sexuality/spirituality education programs for your congregation.

Hancock, Jim, and Kara Powell. *Good Sex 2.0: A Whole-Person Approach to Teenage Sexuality and God.* Grand Rapids: Zondervan, 2009.

Richardson, Justin, and Mark Schuster. *Everything You Never Wanted Your Kids to Know about Sex (But Were Afraid They'd Ask): The Secrets to Surviving Your Child's Sexual Development from Birth to the Teens.* New York: Three Rivers Press, 2003.

# Questions \ for Discussion and Contemplation

1 What sort of formal sex education did you receive? Was it similar to the Eighters' model, or was it different? Did it help you navigate your way through adolescence and young adulthood, or did it hinder your development?

2 What role (if any) should the church have in teaching sex education? Or is this something that should be left to parents and/or schools to teach?

3 If sex education takes place in a church setting, should that education be strictly "abstinence only," or should it provide information on contraception?

4 What do sexuality and spirituality have to do with each other? In your own life, how have sexuality and spirituality affected each other?

wtf?

# Christianity

## What's a Body Got to Do with It?

Chapter 4

*We do not have bodies, as we like to suppose, distancing ourselves from them as one does from an inferior, a servant, who works for us… We are bodies, "body and soul."…If we like the part of ourselves we call 'mind' or 'spirit,' then we ought to honor that part which is its base or root—the body—for they belong together.*[1] • Sallie McFague

### Body Problems

Like countless others in the United States, I have a problem—a body problem. As a clergy woman in general, I study, preach, and teach the gospel. As a youth minister in particular, I minister to and with young people, walking beside them as they journey through faith and culture. Topping my list of pastoral priorities is the task of reminding teenagers and young adults that they are beloved children of God and that they are wonderful physically as well as spiritually. Yet when it comes to my own body, I am far from immune to the pressures of physical perfection as well as the temptation to devalue the body in relation to mind/spirit. My body and I are not friends, and in truth, we haven't been friends for a long time.

When did this estrangement from my physical self begin? While a part of me would like very much to point to adolescence and the tumult that comes with middle-school cruelty in the midst of puberty, if I dig honestly and deeply into my life, I am forced to settle upon late childhood as the birthplace of my body loathing. In this phase of life the fissure began, the break that ultimately left body and mind/spirit as enemies.

The American myth describes childhood as a time of wonder and whimsy, an age when everything is carefree and sadness only interlopes when a beloved pet or grandparent dies, a period when body and spirit/mind soar together. However, for a large number of children, reality bears little resemblance to this story. While my own childhood was mostly an incarnation of the myth (a family that lived with an abundance of love, plenty of food on the table, abuse-free familial interactions, stability, and broad groups of friends who shared my passion for stories, tree climbing, and outdoor adventure), two devastating specters entered into the picture around my ninth year and destroyed much of the wholeness we desire for our children.

I cannot recall which came first—the warped body image or the abuse—and in the grand scheme of things, it does not matter. What does matter is that in the third grade I realized I was overweight, and my best friend's older brother began sexually abusing both of us. As my friend and I watched her brother's pornographic tapes and listened to his instructions on what would be required of us by our boyfriends or husbands, I learned that my body was both ugly and shameful—and when I went home and looked in the mirror at my awkward, pudgy frame, I knew it was true.

Like most children who suffer abuse, I didn't tell my parents. Instinctively I knew that such disclosure would simultaneously hurt my parents and harm my best friend, so I sought to protect them all—and in so doing, I began to widen the fracture inside myself. On the outside I remained the outdoor girl (though I became quieter and more introverted), but on the inside I became depressed and obsessed with achieving the physical "perfection" of those girls on my abuser's VHS tapes. In my decision to keep silent about his abuse, I instead accepted his definition of ideal womanhood and then promptly shut down. It would be another twenty years before the memories of these childhood scars fought their way back to the surface.

Adolescence is never easy. But with my buried hurts, this season of transition was hellish. Already knowing that my body was unacceptable in all its awkward, chubby, spectacled glory, the messages from my peers cut to the heart. I was fat. I was ugly. I was unlovable. Rather than viewing these descriptors as the opinions of less charitable schoolmates, I understood them as Truth. Overweight, ugly, and unlovable did not describe me—I *was* all these things. They were the primary states of my being.

In the summer before my eighth grade year, the playing field changed. A substantial growth spurt left me tall and slender. Contact lenses replaced the coke-bottle lenses, and a bad perm grew out, leaving my blonde hair long and straight. On the first day of school few people recognized me—girls who had tortured me the year prior sought my friendship, and boys who had ignored me now wanted my phone number. My physical transformation had all the hallmarks of a teenage Cinderella story—except that this cinder-girl could not accept the attention. I knew that the attention was false, not because the leopards around me had changed their spots but because I knew I could not possibly be beautiful or desirable.

Eventually, I mellowed and learned to play along. I flirted, made new friends, and dated. But the specters of the past accompanied me everywhere I went. My babysitter had taught me well, and I entered the dating world knowing what men really wanted from a "perfect woman." Detached from my body and knowing that my body was already shameful, bit by bit I acquiesced to what was expected of me. My teenage and young adult years were a long equation comprised of one part self-hatred, one part self-abuse, and one part poor choices—these things ultimately added up to misery.

*self-hatred + self-abuse + poor choices = misery*

### Where Was the Church?

Having already acknowledged, earlier in this essay, that I am a minister, it is only right that one might ask: "Where were God and the church in all of this?" Given the story I have shared, it may come as a surprise to know that throughout my childhood and adolescence, I was an active churchgoer. I believed in God, loved Jesus, and enjoyed participation in the various Disciples churches we attended. Moreover, as a teen, church (and especially church camp) became a haven for me. Within my church family, I knew I was a beloved child of God. I quickly assumed roles of responsibility: presiding over communion at sixteen, singing in the choir, serving as president of the Area Youth Council, and preaching my first sermon at seventeen. In the course of my church life I received a call to ministry, and after high school I headed off to Texas Christian University to study religion and prepare for seminary. In many ways, the church became my life.

Yet in the midst of joyful service and participation, the church also reinforced my broken state. While I knew from the church that I was a loved and chosen child of God, church teachings told me that this primarily applied to my mind/spirit. My body (as well as the bodies of others) was suspect because of its impermanence and its susceptibility to sin. While teachers in my congregation might tell me that my body should be honored as God's temple, they also taught me that I should distrust my body because of its sheer physicality and sinfulness. Rather than offering wholeness, these messages reinforced the truth I already knew about myself: My mind/spirit might be good but my body was very, very bad. Beyond that, I learned I was right to hate my body/physical self because God didn't particularly like it either. In short, church teachings encouraged me to continue living as a broken person.

At thirty-one, newly ordained, nearly a decade of theological education and ministry under my belt, and a husband who loves me in my entirety, I am still not reconciled with my body. I watch the young people in my care as they struggle with body image and their own physicality, and I know that for their sake as well as my own we must radically alter the

> The church reinforced my broken state.

church's witness regarding the body. Wholeness is literally a matter of life and death.

What would happen if the church truly affirmed the God-created beauty and worth of the human body? What would it look like to live in a body of Christ that loves bodies as much as minds and spirits? How would it orient us toward justice in the world if we truly believed that bodily well-being is just as important as mental health and spiritual maturity? One of the ways to answer these questions is to look at the spiritual and practical consequences for centuries of body loathing in the church. By examining these repercussions, we can get a clearer insight into what is at stake when we value mind/spirit at the expense of the body.

### Practical and Theological Consequences

**1. Viewing the mind/spirit and body as separate—and treating the body as less valuable or bad—waters down our ability to stand in solidarity with those who suffer physical abuse and oppression.**

The issue of human suffering should be of paramount concern for the people of God. If the church is to be an agent of hope and change in the world, we must take seriously the physical suffering of those in our homes, towns, nations, and world. So long as the church minimizes the value and God-createdness of the human body, we will look past suffering in our attempts to focus on the mind/spirit of God's children. When we do so, we tell people that the abuse, oppression, and pain they suffer is ultimately inconsequential, and this does not speak to human experience or reality. Victims of abuse and their abusers need to hear that God does not approve of abuse and that God thinks their bodies are as precious as their minds/spirits—and these people need to hear this truth in their Sunday School classes, Bible studies, and directly from the pulpit on Sunday morning. Only when our views of the body change will our witness against abuse become authentic.

God does not approve of abuse!!

**2. Focusing on the mind/spirit at the expense of the body leads many well-intentioned Christians to spiritualize**

the promises of hope made by Jesus in the Sermon on the Mount.

This error has led the church of the ages to tell the poor and meek that "inherit the earth" actually points to otherworldly rewards. When we participate in this type of spiritualization, we root people within their situations of abuse and oppression, encouraging them to "stick it out" patiently instead of resisting and claiming their own God-given dignity. Teachings on the inherent value of the body are crucial if the church is to continue Jesus' tradition of caring for both the physical and spiritual needs of God's people. If the body truly is an inferior thing compared to the mind/spirit, then we could rightly spiritualize all of Jesus' teachings and tell (or continue telling) the poor and marginalized that all is well—while they will receive no relief for their physical suffering, they will receive a spiritual reward in heaven (after the abuse or neglect of others has killed them!). However, if the body and mind/spirit are a total package and are equally valued by God, then part of our call is to stand against all abuse, neglect, and violence—the physical as well as the emotional/spiritual. As theologian Sallie McFague rightly insists: "bodies matter!"[2] And because they matter, our model of the church should not be about the business of individual souls seeking individual salvation.[3] Instead it should be about an entire people, a whole people, working and praying and hoping for corporate salvation: The church should model to the world not that we are a community of individuals seeking salvation, but that we are a whole community seeking salvation and justice for all of creation (physically as well as spiritually).

### 3. When we spiritualize Jesus' teachings, we also spiritualize him as a savior.

When we focus on Jesus as solely divine, we diminish the gift and promise of Emmanuel—God with us. If we cannot accept and love the humanity of Christ alongside his divinity, then we deny God—refusing to let God into the world in its beauty and brokenness. If we deny or deemphasize the humanity of Christ, we continue to keep God estranged from creation and dilute the potency of Christ's salvific nature. Jesus was and is the exemplar of wholeness. He routinely tended to both the physical and mental/spiritual needs of the people with whom he came into contact. This can be seen best in the accounts of Jesus' many miracles: Jesus healed physical ailments such as blindness and leprosy and even death, but also healed people who suffered from mental/spiritual ailments (such as the "exorcism" of Legion [Mk. 5:1-13]). All around, Jesus was concerned with both the physical and mental/spiritual well-being of the people who came into his care. He cared for both the physical and the spiritual equally—just as he was equally human and divine—and ultimately his concern was salvation of whole people.

**4. By denying the value of the human body, we help to maintain our broken state instead of living into and claiming the wholeness that God intended for creation from the beginning.**

When God created human beings out of both dust and breath, the intention was clear: God intended for human beings to be whole—body joined with mind/spirit. However, we learn in the third chapter of Genesis that this wholeness is short-lived. As they contemplate the tree of knowledge of good and evil, the serpent tells Eve the most powerful and irresistible of lies: that the image of God within her is entirely rooted in her mind/spirit and that it is better to pursue the development of her mind/spirit than to care for the body (and the wholeness) given to her by God (Gen. 3:4-6). Taking the bait, Eve eats of the tree and also convinces her partner, Adam, to join her. Once they have both partaken of the fruit of the Tree, the first humans become aware that their bodies are naked and they feel ashamed (Gen. 3:7). Here, for the first time, the human body is perceived as somehow unacceptable. In this moment, the body becomes a source of shame; human beings are now divided creatures rather than whole beings (divided from themselves, one another, and from God). Similarly, whenever we lift one part of our created

> **W**hen we lift mind/spirit above our God-given bodies, we willfully remain broken.

nature above another, we reject God's plan for humanity. In so doing, we willfully remain broken.

**5. A skewed understanding of the human body distorts our understanding of the church as the body of Christ.**

When the apostle Paul wrote to his fledgling assemblies about their membership in the body of Christ, he did so with the knowledge that his audience would understand and value the complex workings and interactions of the human body. In his first letter to the community of believers in Corinth, Paul states:

> But as it is, God arranged the members in the body, each one of them, as he chose. If all were a single member, where would the body be? ... The eye cannot say to the hand, "I have no need of you," nor again the head to the feet, "I have no need of you." On the contrary, the members of the body that seem to be weaker are indispensable, and those members of the body that we think less honorable we clothe with greater honor... God has so arranged the body, giving the greater honor to the inferior member, that there may be no dissension within the body, but the members may have the same care for one another. If one member suffers, all suffer together with it; if one member is honored, all rejoice together with it. (1 Cor. 12:18-26)

The original readers of this letter already had a basic understanding of how the physical body works, so when their teacher and leader compared the church to a human body they not only knew what he meant but also understood that they were to treat both their bodies and one another with respect. Today, a couple thousand years later, as we associate the human body with shame and sin, we destroy our ability to understand and appreciate Paul's metaphor. The more we devalue the body, the more we devalue the church as an instrument of God's grace in a broken world. Paul knew that just as we have flesh, so too is the church made up of bodies. These bodies, yours and mine, make the church a tangible and effective witness to the life, ministry, death, and resurrection of Jesus Christ in a world that desperately needs hope of wholeness.

## Conclusion

Bodies matter! I knew this when I was nine years old, but I learned a twisted version of this truth. I learned that bodies matter because they are imperfect, ugly, and sinful. Through the lessons of abuse, I came to know that bodies matter because they are somehow wrong. In the learning of such bad news, I was not alone. Countless thousands and millions of others have learned the inverse of God's truth regarding the body, and because of it they live lives of suffering, indignity, continued abuse, self-destruction, and misery.

What can the church do about this problem? For starters, it can show up for the discussion. I believe passionately that religious people (teachers, preachers, rabbis, imams, parents, and the like) are the only ones who can correct the body problem that faces our society. But instead of stepping up to the microphone and sharing the good word that bodies matter for positive reasons, religious people have largely given in to the temptation to either agree with prevailing attitudes about the body or (perhaps worse) to reject the body outright by saying that the body doesn't matter at all.

We must boldly counter falsehood with truth. When a nine-year-old believes that her body matters because of the sexual pleasure it can give someone else, she needs her Sunday School teacher to remind her that her body matters because her hug can brighten the day of a friend in need. When a sixteen-year-old thinks that his body was created to take a parent's punches, he needs his preacher to show him that his body was made for joyful service. When a twenty-five or thirty-five-year-old mourns the passing of the valuable body that once fit into that skimpy black dress, she needs a friend to point out that her body was wonderfully made to carry the child she just delivered. And when an eighty-year-old knows his aged frame is no longer of any use, he needs a partner to remind him that every wrinkle and scar carries a story of great value that must be told.

Bodies matter!

Christianity

49

But the acceptance of falsehood tends to silence us. Most victims of abuse never come forward to report what they have suffered. Most who hate what they see in the mirror never share their self-loathing for fear that others will simply confirm their worst fears. Most who mourn the passing of time and aging of frame simply suffer in silence. This silence requires us to act now, speaking and preaching body-truths whenever we can. If we wait until someone asks us for the truth, we will be too late. Our unspoken body problems are truly a matter of life and death, and we must take every opportunity to speak life and light into the darkness.

What's the body got to do with it?

EVERYTHING.

## Bibliography

McFague, Sallie. *The Body of God: An Ecological Theology.* Minneapolis: Fortress Press, 1993.

## Additional Resources

Barger, Lilian Calles. *Eve's Revenge: Women and a Spirituality of the Body.* Ada, Mich.: Brazos Press: 2003.

Brumberg, Joan Jacobs. *The Body Project: An Intimate History of American Girls.* New York: Random House, 1997.

Nelson, James B. *Body Theology.* Louisville: Westminster/John Knox Press, 1992.

Paulsell, Stephanie. *Honoring the Body: Meditations on a Christian Practice.* San Francisco: Jossey-Bass, 2003.

# Questions \ for Discussion and Contemplation

1 What has the church taught you about the body? How does this fit with or oppose what the world teaches you?

2 What would happen if the church truly affirmed the God-created beauty and worth of the human body?

3 What would it look like to be in a church that loved bodies as much as minds and spirits?

4 How could it orient us toward justice in the world if we truly believed that bodily well-being is as important as mental health and spiritual maturity?

5 Where do you see the church (your congregation in particular or the church at large) changing its approach to the human body? Where has it remained the same? How do you feel about these trends?

6 What changes can you make in your own congregation to help young people (as well as adults) learn to view their bodies in healthy ways?

wtf?

# Growing Up Gay

## A Life in the Church

**Chapter 5**

"Can we talk about the church bus now?" Those words, spoken at a church board meeting, were about the sweetest I had ever heard. As a matter of fact, I thought they would make a perfect ending to a movie. Having a flair for the dramatic, I often imagine moments of my life as they would appear on screen, and in the instant I heard that sentence, I could clearly see credits rolling and hear sappy music beginning to play, the camera zooming in on my face as I smiled and looked up toward heaven with grateful relief.

Throughout the previous year, I had worried, prayed, prepared, and finally decided to tell the administrative board at the church where I serve as the music minister that I am gay. I had several reasons for wanting to do this. Because I was also attending seminary at the time and was planning to seek ordination, I felt that it was only fair to be honest with them about the person they were being asked to support through that process. In addition, I thought that being "out of the closet" at work was an important step in my development as an adult. Most importantly, I simply wanted to tell them before they asked—I don't like awkward confrontations.

In the months leading up to this meeting, I had already told the senior staff at the church as well as the group of church members who had been brought together to act as my ministry mentors for a practical theology class at seminary. Although they supported my decision to talk to the board, I still updated my resume in case I was asked to step down from my position.

Walking into the church board meeting that night, I was as stressed as I had been before I had come out to my parents a couple of months before. However, this meeting was to take place in real time, a feat I never worked up the nerve to perform with my parents. I sent them a letter. After I dropped it in the mailbox, I went back to my apartment and threw up.

With both the church and my parents, I had come to terms with the fact that these relationships would be forever altered—perhaps even severed. Although my parents thankfully did not disown me, I think they believed they had failed me in some way. While I had been dealing with my sexual orientation for three decades, they were taken by surprise ("Have they ever met you?" one of my friends asked when I recounted their shock) and asked for some time to get used to the idea.

Telling the church board, on the other hand, was anticlimactic. There was no discussion. There were no questions. Someone made a motion for the church to endorse me as an ordination candidate, there was a second, and the motion was unanimously approved. Then, a request to move on to more urgent matters—exactly how much was the new church bus going to cost?

I was so happy! These church people knew I was gay, and they still wanted me! They still loved me! They thought I was worthy of being an ordained minister. For someone who has spent a large part of his life trying to please other people, this undisputed endorsement of my worth was important to me.

I had not, however, anticipated that this particular church had the slowest rumor mill in the history of Christendom. In the weeks that followed, what I assumed was acceptance by the entire congregation was instead blissful ignorance. The news of my revelation took months to seep slowly throughout the congregation, and the results weren't always pretty. But I'm getting ahead of myself. Before I can adequately recount what happened after this movie-of-the-week moment, I need to elaborate on what happened first. It is a tale of deception, fear, guilt, and shame that led me through several churches and denominations, years of counseling and therapy, and approximately 7,000 packs of cigarettes (a habit I have thankfully ended). In keeping with my movie theme, let's call this the flashback.

### A Child Afraid: The Early Years

Here's a recipe for a challenging childhood: Take one gay child, and place him in the southeastern United States; add a father who honestly could have been the Marlboro Man, a mother with deep and sincere religious convictions, and stir in a rural Free Will Baptist church. Mix well and stand back.

I have always known I am gay. By the time I was six or seven, I was having fantasies about growing up and marrying men. And even though I was in the South, I didn't fully realize that this was not okay until the fourth grade when I was called a faggot for the first time.

Faggot is the slur I most despise. I can handle most of the others—queer, sissy, fairy, homo—even fag, which is, of course, short for faggot. But faggot is different—it sounds so harsh and violent. And it rhymes with maggot. But I digress.

Though I knew it had been said in a derogatory way, I didn't know what the word itself meant, so I asked my parents. They handled it pretty well, meaning they didn't panic or freak out, and they assured me that the kids at school didn't really know what that word meant either. As carefully as they could with a nine-year-old, they described what it meant to be a gay man, and it didn't take me long to realize that this was a horrible thing to be. I was terrified because some of the actions they described were things I had already thought about. Then to give me an example of how these types of people behaved, they offered up the example of a flamboyant man from our neighborhood named Gary who held his cigarettes in a long holder and would often wear his silk pajamas to the local country store. I had heard other adults laugh at him behind his back and refer to him as "Gay-ry." My head swam as I began to put the pieces together. The kids at school thought I was weird like the adults thought Gary was weird, and I didn't own silk pajamas or a cigarette holder. What had I done for them to suspect that I was so different? Could they tell that I wanted a boyfriend and not a girlfriend?

At this point, I had only one course of action available to me. I prayed. I was an ardent pray-er. Having attended church since birth, I carried a deep love for God and for Jesus (though I was afraid of the Holy Ghost) and trusted them to see me through tough times. Because I hadn't grasped the concept that the three parts of the Trinity are just one God, I followed the advice of my Sunday school teacher: to pray to Jesus for everyday needs and appeal to God only when something was really important. This was a problem that required a direct line to God.

Starting that night, I would fill the prayer-line to God with fervent prayers for many years to come. I had become a child afraid. I knew I hadn't asked to have the feelings I did, but because I did have them, I came to believe that God must have given them to me as a test (I had paid close attention to the story of Job). I shuddered to think what else God might send my way to try my faith if I failed.

I was afraid of being stabbed in the middle of the night, of being kidnapped, of being beaten up by the bully at school, of failing my grade, and of missing the rapture. I was most afraid, however, of being different in general and of being gay in particular. I didn't want to be laughed at and made fun of and called names. Instead, I just wanted to fit in and be like everybody else.

The only place I didn't mind standing out was at church. There, I felt special and accepted. Despite my fear that God was testing me, I was truly able to experience God's love in that little Baptist church—especially when we were singing hymns. Music became an important part of my life because of the church. At school, they made fun of me because I liked to sing and play the piano. At church those talents were nurtured and encouraged.

I believe the best that life has to offer comes in moments of pure, unadulterated joy. For me, I first found those moments in music—looking up at the knotty pine ceiling of that tiny country church, singing hymns by heart with a roomful of people who loved God and who loved me. I grew older, however, and those moments of joy came with less regularity because I suspected the love I felt was conditional. I was beginning to realize that my physical attraction to men was not being taken away by prayer. Would my church family still love me if they knew my secret? Would my parents? Would God? As usual, I was afraid—afraid the answer was no.

### Nose in a Book: Adolescence

Reading is my favorite pastime and has been ever since I learned how. My favorite books when I was a kid were the Little House books (I envied the adventurous nature of the pioneers—and I loved to hate Nellie Oleson) and the Nancy Drew books (even though my seventh grade social studies teacher announced to the entire class that I should be reading the Hardy Boys instead). I think what resonated with me in these books was that both Laura Ingalls and Nancy Drew were girls who did extraordinary things. While I couldn't identify with being a girl per se, I could relate to being considered less valuable than my peers for no clear reason. Sure I was awful at sports, but as a student I was well behaved and made good grades. Yet having a high grade point average or being able to play the piano somehow does not equate with making touchdowns on the basketball court—I always get that wrong. I meant to say football court. And so to escape, I read.

As a good Baptist, I also read the Bible (the King James Version), but that wasn't escape reading. This reading was research to assist me in figuring out the gravity of my sins. I learned that being gay was sinful:

> Thou shalt not lie with mankind, as with womankind: it is abomination. (Lev. 18:22, KJV)

> For this cause God gave them up unto vile affections... the men, leaving the natural use of the woman burned in their lust toward one another; men with men working that which is unseemly. (Rom. 1:26–27, KJV)

Fantasizing was sinful:

But I say unto you, That whosoever looketh on a woman to lust after her hath committed adultery with her already in his heart. (Mt. 5:28, KJV)

Masturbation was sinful:

[Onan] spilled his semen on the ground to keep from producing offspring for hisbrother. What he did was wicked in the LORD's sight; so he put him to death also. (Gen. 38:9–10, NIV)

And then, there was the granddaddy of all of the scary texts:

Wherefore I say unto you, All manner of sin and blasphemy shall be forgiven unto men: but the blasphemy against the Holy Ghost shall not be forgiven... whosoever speaketh against the Holy Ghost, it shall not be forgiven him, neither in this world, neither in the world to come. (Mt. 12:31–32, KJV)

Although I wasn't sure I knew what this "unforgivable sin" was, I was relatively confident I had committed it by promising God I would stop masturbating or daydreaming about sex, and then doing it repeatedly.

My soul was tortured with the thought of eternal damnation. Being in middle school is hard enough, with hormones raging and acne marching across the face like little red soldiers, but dealing with all of that while believing you are bound for hell is almost too much to handle!

As I entered high school, much of the country's attention turned to the growing AIDS crisis. Here was yet another thing to be afraid of, and many rumors swirled around about the disease and how it was transmitted—we even worried we might catch it from mosquitoes. AIDS had also caused a huge backlash against gays, who were blamed for creating and spreading it. I was a fourteen-year-old virgin who felt guilty for bringing AIDS to the world because of my horrendous thoughts!

With all that I heard from the media and the pulpit, my peers and my mentors, I had no doubt that being a homosexual was one of the worst sins possible. Through it all, however, I continued to pray and go to church, hoping for a miracle that one morning I would wake up and be straight. But my faith that such a miracle would occur waned with each passing year as my desire for male companionship grew. Because I knew I could never act on those feelings, I dated a few girls when I was in high school. No lasting relationship evolved out of those dates, but they did help me feel a little more normal (as did the smoking habit I picked up). However, I was still extremely curious about what the male body looked like, and I briefly considered becoming a doctor just so I could see pictures of nude men without the shame associated with buying a copy of *Playgirl*. This was my level of maturity as I entered college.

### Truth and Consequences: The College Years

A crush, yes. Infatuation, yes. But my freshman year in college marked the first time I had ever fallen head-over-heels in love. I thought he was perfect. We spent a lot of time together, and though he dated girls, he flirted with me too. "God," I prayed, "please let him kiss me. And please don't let me go to hell for praying for you to help me sin. Is this feeling a sin?"

He never did kiss me, but for the first time, I decided to seek help for my "problem." I met with the campus minister at the Baptist-affiliated college I had chosen to attend, and he assured me that these feelings were mere curiosity. Deviant sexual desires were created to be squelched. "Just because I may find a rape scene in a movie arousing," he said, "doesn't make me a rapist." Ummm, OK.

As long as I participated in trying to become heterosexual, we had a great relationship. But I wasn't getting any better. I stopped eating and lost about forty pounds in one semester. I knew I could not continue in this way, and finally I told him I needed to face the fact that I was gay. His attitude changed completely. "Well, the Bible condemns it," he said at our final meeting. I was heartbroken. Not only was I going to hell for something I couldn't help, but someone I had trusted with my deepest secret had turned off the switch on our relationship. I never saw him again.

In the meantime, I had left the Free Will Baptist Church, deciding that Catholicism was the way to go. I began attending a tiny parish in town and became friends with the priest. In this church, I rediscovered those moments of joy that had all but disappeared from my life. In the liturgy and ancient prayers of the Catholic Church, I felt security. I loved the rituals of kneeling, of crossing oneself, of sharing holy water. And for the first time I thought I might actually be able to serve as a minister. This was a desire I had kept secret for a long time, because I believed myself too sinful to pursue it. But since Catholic priests are celibate, I reasoned, my sexual desires wouldn't be an issue.

I put some serious research and prayer into this idea, but I soon moved from this small college town to a university in a larger city. My horizons began to broaden as I met people who weren't necessarily Baptist, Catholic, or even religious. Then, one day in the university newspaper, I saw an advertisement for a support group for gay and lesbian students. I wasn't sure what kind of support they were offering, but I was certainly intrigued. Maybe others who struggled with the same issues could provide some insight.

When I stepped into the meeting room that afternoon, I guess I was expecting to see limp-wristed guys flitting around while flannel-wearing gals adjusted carburetors. Instead, I saw regular-looking young women and men, laughing and talking. I was surprised at how normal they were. What surprised me even more was that the staff sponsor was a lesbian minister. It was hard enough to wrap my mind around the idea of a woman minister, much less one who openly admitted she was attracted to other women!

Paranoid to the extreme, I used a fake name to introduce myself to the group, but I attended faithfully every week. When I told the sponsor of my desire to be a minister, she gave me a book that changed my life: *Uncommon Calling* by Chris Glaser. In the book, Glaser describes his struggle to become an openly gay minister in the 1970s.

By then believing all ability to love ultimately comes from God, I felt led to the conclusion my sexual orientation was a gift from God. Like all of God's gifts, my choice was whether to reject it or accept and invest it as a good steward. I could hide it like the servant in the parable, who took the coin his master had given him and hid it in the dirt, or I could use it wisely as the faithful steward did for the master's glory and the benefit of all.[1]

My sexuality might be a gift? I felt a double flood of relief and anxiety as I pondered that phrase over and over again. If this were true, I thought, my troubles were over. At the same time, such an idea was too good to be true, so I felt guilty for even entertaining its verity.

Finally, for better or worse, I made up my mind to come clean about all the secrets consuming my life. First, I told my support group I had been using a fake name. I assumed my new friends would understand why I had done it, but they felt betrayed, and I was never able to fully fit in with them again. I gradually stopped attending. I also told my priest I was gay. "You're not gay! You're not gay!" He spat those words at me as if they tasted rotten in his mouth, and I never saw him again.

I returned to the closet having learned a valuable lesson: Tell the truth, and people reject you.

### Working It Out: Adulthood

After college, I worked in an office or two, and flip-flopped between my desire to be openly gay and my desire for safety. I had seen all too many times that being openly gay increased your chances of being beaten up. I didn't date often for fear of being discovered. Over the years, I told a few friends my secret, and I found some comfort in being able to be myself with them. I felt an ever-present anxiety, however, of the power these friends had over me. I thought if I made them mad, they would tell my secret and ruin my life. The last thing I wanted was for my parents to find out, so I went out of my way to please everyone.

I took a job as a Sundays-only pianist at a small Disciples of Christ church near where my parents lived. I really liked the people and the theology expressed from the pulpit, and within a few years, I told the minister that I was gay and that I wanted to be a minister. He could not have been more supportive, and he opened my eyes to different ways of interpreting scripture.

My sexuality may be a gift.

Growing Up Gay

Such a shift in thinking helped me see the world from new angles, and though I still felt guilty and afraid, I was also learning to become grateful for the gifts and talents God had given to me.

Filled with verve, I applied to seminary and was accepted. Leaving my Southern home and family was difficult, but I was confident that I would finally "find myself" in Texas—that bastion of liberalism. And I did.

I entered seminary as an openly gay man. I received fantastic support from my new friends and professors, and I felt for the first time that I was truly worthy of being called to the ministry of Jesus Christ. As I worked on my master's degree, I was able to interact with extremely intelligent people, professors and students alike, who believed that the term "gay Christian" was not an oxymoron. I entered counseling to help me deal with many of my issues of guilt and fear, and I came out of that process a much happier and more confident person. So much that I decided to pursue ordination as an openly gay man, which brings us back to where we started.

*I was able to interact with people who believed "gay Christian" was not an oxymoron*

**The Story Continues**

I'm not sure anyone on the church board that night said anything about my sexual orientation outside of that meeting. While many churches are really good at spreading gossip, this one was not, and it literally took months for the news to get around. That was when some people began to leave the congregation. One day while making a hospital visit, I ran into a woman who had resigned her membership. "I hope you didn't take it personally," she said. Well, how else should one take it when people leave their church because of you?

The local church leadership was wonderfully encouraging of my ministry even as members left and as I was denied entrance into the ordination process because of my sexual orientation— or rather for my insistence to talk about it as an important part of my call to ministry.

The larger church does not like to talk about homosexuality because the church has never learned to talk in a healthy way about sex in general. I think the problem many Christians have with homosexuality does not lie primarily in the fact that two people of the same gender can find companionship or love with each other. The problem exists in misguided and archaic ideas about the sexual act itself.

In her book *Body, Sex, and Pleasure*, Christine Gudorf explains that, for centuries the church has deemed sexual pleasure evil and has expected good Christians to perform their marital duties with the least possible pleasure.[2] When two people of the same sex engage in sexual activity, the main outcome desired is sexual satisfaction. The idea of sex as an expression of love or just for fun, even between committed couples, scares the church.

Gudorf also insists that we learn to separate sex and procreation, because "it denigrates sexual relationships in which coitus is not possible."[3] Gay sex is most often condemned because it is impossible for two people of the same gender to conceive a child. So what? It is also impossible to conceive a child through oral sex or while using effective contraception. Until I am assured that all opponents of the so-called "gay lifestyle" are having penile-vaginal sex without foreplay for the sole purpose of having children, I will turn a deaf ear to their arguments.

*As much as gay people are caricatured, we are simply people.*

I also tire of hearing the stereotype that gay people are overly promiscuous. Gay people are often portrayed as sex-crazed animals who seek sex wherever they can find it and who care nothing for other people's feelings so long as their own sexual desires are met. Some gay people are promiscuous; others aren't—just like straight people.

That is the fact many in the church fail or refuse to understand: As much as gay people are analyzed and caricatured, we are simply people. We are created by God and in God's image—just like straight people. We are capable of doing good and evil—just like straight people. We love and worry and cry and sweat—just like straight people.

But instead of being seen as regular people, we are often looked upon as different, as other. I think dealing with lifelong intolerance gives the gay community the ability to draw closer together. I am lucky enough to have many good friends in my life, and I love them all, but I experience a level of sameness with my gay friends that frees me from my entrenched fear of judgment and returns to me my moments of pure joy.

To have the freedom to worship and work and live freely is a basic human right. With so many fighting for such freedom in the world, how could the church even consider denying full participation to any single group of people inside—or outside—its walls? Yet the church does just that whenever it is complacent about issues of injustice, when it denies ordination based on sexual orientation, and when it flagrantly persecutes or judges others. By demanding silence from a large portion of the population, the dying church is rejecting a lifeline of creativity, energy, and hope. In the process it is effectively destroying itself.

How awful that as an adult I so rarely experience that life essence of pure joy in the church. I think many gay people are reticent to truly be themselves in church unless the congregation is forthright about its openness. I am grateful for churches that are gay-friendly or that are designated as "open and affirming" because these are safe places for gay people to worship and to hear words that are so important: God loves you; you are okay; you are accepted. So why does a church have to have a special label to advocate that most basic Christian principle?

Perhaps one day I'll have another perfect movie ending to orchestrate in my head. On that day, the "issue" of homosexuality in the church will disappear. Not because there are no more gay people or because there is no more church, but because it simply won't matter one way or the other.

## Bibliography

Glaser, Chris. *Uncommon Calling: A Gay Christian's Struggle to Serve the Church.* Louisville: Westminster / John Knox Press, 1988.

Gudorf, Christine E. *Body, Sex, and Pleasure: Reconstructing Christian Sexual Ethics.* Cleveland: The Pilgrim Press, 1994.

## Additional Resources

Bawer, Bruce. *A Place at the Table: The Gay Individual in American Society.* New York: Poseidon Press, 1993.

Hardin, Kimeron N. *The Gay and Lesbian Self-Esteem Book: A Guide to Loving Ourselves.* Oakland, Calif.: New Harbinger Publications, 1999.

Kaufman, Gershen, and Lev Raphael. *Coming out of Shame: Transforming Gay and Lesbian Lives.* New York: Doubleday, 1996.

Mixner, David, and Dennis Bailey. *Brave Journeys: Profiles in Gay and Lesbian Courage.* New York: Bantam, 2000.

Growing Up Gay

# Questions \ for Discussion and Contemplation

**1** Do you believe that sexual orientation (heterosexuality, homosexuality, etc.) is a gift from God? Why or why not? Do you believe that homosexuality is a choice?

**2** Shannon states that: "The larger church does not like to talk about homosexuality because the church has never learned to talk in a healthy way about sex in general." Does this statement mesh with your experience, or is it contrary to that experience?

**3** Is the sole purpose of sexual intercourse reproduction? Or does sexuality (and sexual acts) have other God-given purposes?

**4** Why might individuals believe that gays and lesbians threaten the security of the "traditional family"?

**5** Will the issue of homosexuality ever disappear in the church?

**6** In what ways can the church become open to all people?

## Chapter 6

## Porn Nation

When I was a kid, young enough that I was still in preschool, my dad brought a book home for me called *SHOW ME*.[1] It was an oversized, hardcover book with a picture of two naked kids, no more than eight years old, on the cover. The book was all in black and white with big, glossy pictures on every page. It was meant to be educational, assembled by some doctors and therapists in the early seventies, but it left nothing unsatisfied for a young, curious mind.

From boys and girls investigating one another's parts to adults masturbating, men groping men and women kissing women, *SHOW ME* had it all. It even included people—ahem—deeply engaged in sexual acts, and a woman birthing the byproduct of said act. I went from hardly knowing the differences between boys and girls to practically acquiring my graduate degree in gynecological studies overnight.

I was not entirely sure what I was seeing in some of these images that were half as big as I was, but I knew I liked looking at them. By getting me the book, I think my parents intended to cast off any shame that might be associated with the human body and sexuality. While I certainly did not equate anything on my person with shame, I also was more than a little overwhelmed by the brutally matter-of-fact photographs.

I should also mention that my dad was—and is, I suppose—a lifetime subscriber to *Playboy* magazine. These were left around the house, right next to *People* and the newspaper, and I was allowed to peruse them any time I wished. I remember one time around kindergarten when I was sitting in my dad's leather armchair, browsing the Playmate of the Month. I felt so grown up, just like my dad, minus the cigarettes and glass of soda.

But I wasn't grown up; I was five years old.

At the time, a girl in my neighborhood spent a lot of time cruising the greenbelt, which was the semi-enclosed park area in the middle of our small planned community. Her mom was divorced and worked a lot, so she was left to take care of herself most days. She and I spent a good deal of time together.

I didn't really understand much about her mom back then, though now she would likely be called a cougar (a term for older women who have a thing for young guys). Mind you, she never did anything inappropriate with me, but she just possessed this tangible sexuality that dripped from her, and clearly her daughter picked up on it. She would come over to play on the swing set in my back yard and would end up doing stripteases while I sat, staring in bewilderment. And I mean she went all the way down to the goods God gave her and nothing else. If I needed any confirmation that the anatomy presented in the *SHOW ME* book was accurate, she provided it.

I found my mind swimming with all of this input, not quite sure what to do with it all, but it certainly helped me develop what I would consider a premature fascination with things well beyond my emotional maturity level. I had a preschool teacher with enormous breasts, and I was practically hypnotized with curiosity, wondering if they looked anything like the ones in *Playboy*, only much bigger.

Later on I learned what happened to all of those magazines my dad amassed over the years. Old *Playboys* don't die; they just go into hibernation in a drawer somewhere. I didn't learn of the magazines' whereabouts until one year, just before I turned thirteen, when I was home alone the whole summer vacation and cruising the house for something to do.

Do you remember the look on Jed Clampett's face when he shot at some critter on the ground and instead discovered a massive oil well just below the earth's surface? I think that was pretty much the look on my face when I came across more than twenty years of old girlie mags. Suffice it to say that I didn't lack for diversion for some time after that. However, I got to thinking: If he keeps this many magazines around, what else might there be? I dug through the videos on the racks, looking for titles that seemed scintillating and popped them in the VCR. We had all of the early premium cable channels that ran the "soft core" skin flicks at night to keep subscribers interested. Not to disappoint, my dad had dozens of them on tape.

Score.

Why bother with static pictures, after all, when there's Lady Chatterley doing the real deal on video? I think I gained at least fifteen pounds that summer and was probably so white I was nearly translucent by the time I went back to school. The great outdoors had nothing on late night Cinemax videos.

When I'd go to church, the preacher would talk about the evils of sexual profligacy, and I was pretty sure he was aiming his words directly at me. The problem was that the stuff was right there when I went home. Frankly, the guilt he piled on me on Sundays was not a strong enough antidote to keep me from going back to the magazines and videos a few days later.

Maybe I was a terrible, disgusting person for liking this stuff, but by then, it was a part of my reality. I wasn't sure how to just lay it down and pretend it wasn't there. I certainly couldn't go to my pastor or youth leader to talk about it because the anger and shame around issues of sexuality were palpable in my church. The last thing I wanted was more guilt. My mom was the one who took me to church, but she knew perfectly well that this stuff was all over the house.

So was it acceptable or wasn't it? And who in the hell could I possibly confide in to sort it all out?

## The Great Cover-Up

Imagine walking into a sanctuary and, instead of a cross or crucifix hanging before the altar or over the baptistry, you find a painting of Mary, breast exposed, nursing the baby Jesus.

For about fourteen hundred years following Jesus' life, this was more common than most people might realize. Though today it's hard to imagine viewing a naked female breast in a place of worship as being appropriate, this hang-up we have about the human form is a relatively new invention. So what happened?

A fascinating article in *Christian Century*[2] addresses this question, and the answers challenge many of our preconceptions about the symbols we so fervently embrace today. For more than eleven hundred years, the employment of a cross to represent God's love and grace for humanity was much more of a controversial subject than it is today. Because the symbol was so closely associated with violence and criminal activity, many believed it did not evoke the sense of worshipfulness the church sought to impart to its faithful. Not until Anselm and his peers in the twelfth century began to emphasize the notion that Jesus' death specifically was the focal point of God's redemptive acts did the cross take on greater significance in the church. Before this, the death of Jesus was not singled out as any more important to human salvation than the entirety of Christ's life including birth, death, resurrection, and everything in between.

With this new emphasis, Paul's scriptures in the New Testament took on new importance, represented symbolically by the cross. However, for several hundred years following, the cross did not supplant images of the nursing virgin. Rather it coexisted alongside them. In fact during the medieval period when so many suffered from disease and malnutrition, the image of Mary nursing represented God's provision and sustenance, which so many longed for. Even such notable theologians as Clement, Anselm, Augustine, and others depicted "Christian nourishment as coming from God's breasts," according to this article.

A couple of things took place to change our perception of the propriety of the female breast as an image of worship into an object of lust and shame that should be concealed. First, the invention of the printing press made available to the masses all sorts of new information. And much like we've seen with the employment of the Internet to purvey pornography, wherever the dissemination of information is democratized, you'll find smut. Suddenly, we were aware of our nakedness, and what once was adored now seemed dirty.

Second, science progressed to the point that human autopsies became increasingly common. As we began to learn in greater detail the machinations of our own guts, some of the mystery held about the human body began to fall away. Instead of the whole incarnation of ourselves being a holy thing, the body became mere housing for the soul: a piece of meat instead of an inscrutable sanctuary.

In an age where the mysteries of life are explained more and more often by science, and as explicit sexual imagery imposes itself in even more corners of our daily lives, I can't help but think about the direct relationship all of this has to our apparent shame about bringing our whole selves to worship. Why would God have any interest in a part of me that others may perceive as fuel for lust? Perhaps it's in everyone's best interest if I leave that part of me at the church doors.

Better yet, let's go a step further and not only eradicate any images of exposed human flesh from our houses of worship. Let's also make sure that any talk of sexuality or embodied spirituality is considered taboo in the presence of God.

### Digital Sex

Things have only progressed—if you can call it that—with respect to the proliferation of sexually explicit imagery beyond the church walls since then. What began with the printing press found new life when videotape replaced film as the primary medium for producing X-rated movies. What once required audiences to venture out to a grungy movie theater with sticky floors now could be delivered to your doorstep in a discreet package. Cable and satellite TV made access to such content even easier and more anonymous in the eighties, followed by an exponential growth with the advent of the World Wide Web.

When I type the word *porn* into Google, more than 245 million links pop up, offering to fulfill any fetish or curiosity

I can imagine with the single click of a button. I get dozens of e-mails on at least a daily basis, offering to do everything from increasing my genital girth to sending me a mail-order bride from Eastern Europe. I recently added Skype, a Web-based phone service, to my laptop. Now hardly a day goes by that I don't get someone with a name like Daisy Humpsalot or Carmen Iwannalaya sending me a request to hook up.

We all know that sexually explicit images are widely available, but not until I had kids did I realize how incredibly unavoidable they are. Network television commercials include things that make me uncomfortable to watch with my five-year-old son. When I took him to the grocery store the other day, he became transfixed by the *Sports Illustrated* swimsuit edition, placed right at his eye level. On the cover was a bronzed model in one of the tiniest bikinis I've ever seen, and she was pulling one side of the bikini bottom down below her hip, revealing even more of what little she previously had covered.

When I was growing up, plenty of kids didn't have the kind of access to graphic sexual material that I did. But now it's not just a matter of whether or not you bring such materials into your home; keeping such material at arm's length takes an act of constant will, and the efficacy of that is even questionable.

### Body as Temple

Considering the current trends in how many young people treat their bodies and how the oppression of human sexuality has only driven it underground, this puritanical exercise of ours as the church has been nothing less than a disaster. In some ways this has made sexuality all the more fascinating. And the longer we pretend to ignore the normalization of sexual imagery and behavior that is degrading or damaging to the bodies given to us by God, the more risk there is of unaddressed sexual addiction, abuse, body image disorders, and greater hopelessness for a remedy.

It's far easier for churches to take strong positions on issues like homosexuality or abortion than it is to deal with sexual addiction, teen pregnancy risks, eating disorders, and how we as

> This puritanical exercise of ours has been a disaster.

people of faith are responsible to present a voice of healing and hope. It's more convenient to cast plenary judgments on some vague entity out there called *pornography* than to ask harder questions, like:

- What is pornography to you?

- Is there a time and place in which sexually explicit materials, used by consenting adults, is acceptable?

- What about the people producing the sexual content? How do we define *consent*? Is a man or woman in an adult video consenting because they're willing to let people film them engaged in sexual acts for money?

- How about the *Sports Illustrated* swimsuit issue? Is such a product a result of consensual adults? Is it healthy? If not, why not?

- And how about Hollywood? If a Cate Blanchett agrees to perform a nude scene in an award-winning film, for which she is paid millions of dollars, is this explicit? Is it healthy? What good might it do? What damage might it inflict, and upon whom?

- In what contexts are certain materials and images acceptable, and when do they become unacceptable?

If you'll notice, the questions above focus less on passing moral judgment and more on facilitating open dialogue. If those we serve and others in the community cannot feel safe coming to their spiritual leaders to discuss their own questions, confusions, problems, and concerns surrounding sexuality, where do we expect them to go?

*dialogue, not judgment*

I was rather amazed that, although my wife spent almost four years in seminary, she was not required to take a single class specifically related to sexuality. She was sent into the field of active ministry with no particular tools to facilitate healthy dialogue around sexuality, let alone to help her deal with problems having anything to do with sex or sexuality.

When we had a man come to our church who wished to worship with us, but who was still on probation for a sexually-related crime with a minor, we had to improvise. As a church we had to ask ourselves: Can we possibly turn this person away?

If not, how do we ensure the safety of our children? What if some folks in the congregation find out about his past and leave the church because of it?

Most people, no matter their age, have had little or no education on matters of sex, sexuality, and embodiment. They hardly know how to talk to their own spouses about it, let alone their pastors, friends, or fellow congregants. And church leaders can't simply reintroduce what we deem as healthy images of the human body and sexuality into faith communities without equipping people with the tools they need to process it. Indeed, this work would not only require gentle introduction over time, but also a willingness on the part of the people of faith to do the good work of exploring the issue. This willingness can and will take years to nurture, combined with a shared commitment to do the difficult work of exploring sexuality together over time.

Scripture certainly includes examples we can use as points of reference if we choose to use them as such. For example, what does the Song of Solomon portray about human sexuality? What is relatable to us today when we read about David spying on Bathsheba, bathing in the house next door? What exactly is meant by the term *sodomy* in the Bible, and how was it used as a military weapon, versus a means of sexual expression? Naturally, such content can make anyone squirm a bit, but if not here within our faith communities, then where? If not now, when?

What we need is to go all the way back to the beginning and start over. We cannot assume previous knowledge, or that the knowledge most of us have cherry-picked along the way is even accurate or conducive to healthy personal sexuality. People are uncomfortable talking about this stuff because we've successfully demonized practically every expression of sexuality. Meanwhile we ignore the reality of a world struggling with these same issues right in front of our noses.

> We've successfully demonized practically every expression of sexuality.

It's easier to cast judgment, to tell people what to do and what not to do, or to try and delineate between what is supposedly right and wrong. Every person ultimately is responsible for his or her own sexual identity, the materials they consume, and the ways in which they express themselves as embodied sexual beings. By ignoring this vast and complex dimension of human nature, we risk irrelevance at best; at worst we utterly fail to minister to a world in need. By standing in judgment and tossing about superficial standards of piety or moral superiority, we only feed the guilt and confusion so many bear every hour of every day already.

So who's ready to talk about sex?

## Bibliography

McBride, Will. *Show Me!: A Picture Book of Sex for Children and Parents.* New York: St. Martins Press, 1975.

Miles, Margaret R. "God's Love, Mother's Milk," in *Christian Century,* Jan 29, 2008.

## Additional Resources

CLER Ministries (www.clerministries.org), "Comprehensive sexuality education programs offered in churches throughout the United States."

Countryman, L. William. *Dirt, Greed, and Sex: Sexual Ethics in the New Testament and Their Implications for Today.* Minneapolis: Fortress Press, 2007.

Thelos, Philo. *Divine Sex: Liberating Sex from Religious Tradition.* Bloomington, Ill.: Trafford Publishing, 2006.

# Questions \ for Discussion and Contemplation

**1** What is your definition of pornography?

**2** Is there a time and place in which sexually explicit materials, used by consenting adults, is acceptable?

**3** What about the people producing the sexual content? How do we define *consent*? Is a man or woman in an adult video "consenting" because he or she is willing to be filmed engaging in sexual acts for money?

**4** When do sexually-themed images in mainstream fashion and culture magazines, Hollywood movies, and advertising cross the line of appropriateness for you? Do you see these images as generally healthy? Are they realistic? Are they damaging? Why, or why not?

**5** Is it possible for someone to do nude or sexually-oriented scenes in media consensually? Does someone getting paid to do it change the nature of the consent?

**6** When, if ever, is nudity in media appropriate? In what contexts are certain materials and images acceptable, and when do they become unacceptable?

# Shelli R. Yoder

## The Perfect Chase

## Chapter 7

What time is it? 3:00 p.m. Dinner isn't for another two hours, but I'm hungry now. I can't eat. I just ate lunch three hours ago. How can I be hungry already? Better yet, why am I hungry? It was a big lunch at that. I had three bites of my turkey sandwich—pretty big bites too—at least 50 calories a bite. It was a plain sandwich. No mayo. No cheese. Just turkey. So I'll say 150 calories total. I also had tomato soup. I didn't eat it, but I did put my spoon into the bowl and licked the spoon. That is at least 20 calories. Did I lick the spoon once or twice? I'll say twice to be safe. So it's 190 total calories so far today. Oh yeah, the diet soda. That has to have some calories. I know it says zero but please. It's not air. It has to have at least 100 calories. 290. I also had dry cereal for breakfast: a half cup of Grape Nuts without milk—150 calories at least. That puts me at 440. I'll never stay under 500 if I'm still looking at having to eat dinner. And I'm going to have to eat something because I'm going out with the girls. What do I do? If I eat something now, I guess I could cancel going out...again. I could say I am sick or something. Actually if I don't eat the rest of the day and can make it until tomorrow morning then I can reward myself with breakfast. I can't wait that long. Who am I kidding?

My stupid body won't shut up about being hungry. Guess I'll let the girls know I can't make it tonight. But I'm still hungry now. I'll work out. I can burn at least 200 calories running 3 miles. That way I can have another bowl of Grape Nuts for dinner, maybe with milk. We'll see how the run goes. I can't forget to call the girls and cancel. Better yet, I'll send a text.

### The Games We Play

And so go the games we play to fool ourselves that we are in control. Sometimes it looks like a numbers game: counting calories and fat grams; worshiping digits on the scale. Keeping track of miles run and weights lifted. But really it is more like the game of chase. Around and around we go chasing the perfect body: the body that will attract the right guy, the great job, and the successful life; the body that will bring us our best self; the body that will bring us a life worth living; the body that will redeem our existence.

Or so our culture promises. It preaches that we can achieve the ideal body if only we have enough dedication and discipline (and money doesn't hurt). This promise is predicated upon us spending billions of dollars on beauty products and weight loss programs. This promise relies upon our failure to trust our body just as it is. Before we can cash in on the promise of that perfect body, we must first believe our body makes us lazy, unhappy, and unsuccessful. First, blame the body for all the things that aren't going well in your life—a breakup, loss of a job, or loss of meaning and purpose—and then turn to your body to fix it.

Our understanding of who we are is very much informed by our body image. Thousands of times every day we are reminded that who we are is not OK. Thousands of images throughout the Internet, television, magazines, and movies communicate in slick and sexy ways that each of us is inadequate. Just as we are, apparently, none of us is enough. Women and girls are constantly bombarded with messages suggesting that they are, in some sense, unfinished and lacking in some physical way. And with the infamous black and white marketing campaign of retailer Abercrombie and Fitch and *Men's Health* magazine's impossibly ripped cover models, adolescent boys and middle-aged men are no longer immune. Regardless of our gender, we are constantly reminded that our life is nowhere near perfect, nor will it be until our body looks a little more like that. We could be happy and fulfilled if only our body was a little more toned, a tad more tanned, and a little less wrinkled. And so the chase goes on.

Consider this recent thread I came across on "Amy Hillenbrand's" Facebook page. "Amy" is a former beauty pageant participant, and she had recently posted a full body photo of herself in an evening gown from her pageant days—just a few years ago. With all the names and dates changed, here's the verbatim dialogue:

Michael Jones at 5:04pm March 11
    I'm sorry, but this pic is just HOT! LOL!

Jill Smith at 9:02am March 13
    WOW—WOW—WOW This is the most incredibly gorgeous picture I have ever seen of you. Simply stunning!!!!

Amy Hillenbrand at 8:19pm March 15
    A few pounds ago. Hahaha :)

Jill Smith at 8:28pm March 15
    Oh shush! You still look like that! Just with shorter hair and bangs!

Michael Jones at 8:43pm March 15
    She wants me.

Amy Hillenbrand at 9:03pm March 15
    I want her! That's why I'm chasing her on the treadmill everyday! Hahaha

Jill Smith at 4:39am March 16
    Well, I think you are about to catch her!! :) If you join us at the gym at 6:00 AM on M-W-F you will catch up to her by next week!!!

Morgan Childs at 8:57am March 16
    Okay I love the pic!! I know the feeling!! I have a few of these that I have been trying to catch up to also!! Three kids later & for some reason they have left me in the dust!! You on the other hand haven't changed a bit!! U look awesome girl!! Enjoy being young & gorgeous!!!

### The Lost and Found Prodigal

In the fifteenth chapter of Luke's gospel, we encounter a classic story about being tempted by that which lies outside of one's true self, chasing that which we are told will fill us up, and ending up completely empty. In the parable of the prodigal, we meet a guy who leaves home and journeys to a distant country in search of glamour and glitz. However, life in the fast lane quickly puts this guy into the ditch. We are told he runs out of money and out of options, and winds up with a job feeding pigs. Daydreaming about stealing some of the pig food, his body tells him he is starving. And so does his soul. Eventually he comes to his senses and remembers that his father has plenty of food and boundless grace. And so we are told that he returned home to his father, who greeted him with open arms and a joyful declaration that his son "was lost and is found" (Lk. 15:24).

In the biblical text, the decision to return home is wrapped up a little too neatly. In reality, the decision to be faithful and to listen to what our body is saying is not easy. Frankly, just like the prodigal, we all chase emptiness. Whether it's a diet fad or a wrinkle cream, who hasn't wondered if life would be better if the body were five pounds lighter and the skin a little smoother around the eyes? In fact, we are all chasing an empty ideal that lies outside of ourselves, and we must constantly recommit to going home to that inner place where we can reconnect with our authentic self. In order to be true to who we are—regardless of our size and shape—we must be intentional about coming to our senses and keeping connected to the truth and power that resides deep within. Returning to that inward home, as the prodigal story points out, is where we receive the greatest welcome and experience the genuine liberation that frees to us live an authentic, connected, and purposeful life.

The quest for authenticity, however, must be entered into again and again and again, particularly because we are constantly changing and evolving along individual journeys. For instance, no one is the same person in fifth grade that she is during her freshman year in college. Consider the twelve-year-old girl who wakes up one day and, all of a sudden, has become self-conscious. She stops participating in sports. She

*Frankly, we all chase emptiness.*

stops raising her hand in class. She leaves "home"—that is, the certainty and comfort of being exactly who she is supposed to be—and goes searching "in a distant country" for authenticity and identity and perfection and whatever else she now believes she lacks. She might turn to the cosmetic department at Macy's, the latest celebrity diet profiled in *InStyle* magazine, or the fitness equipment at the local YMCA. Tragically, she has embarked upon a potentially never-ending exploration of this distant country—an external pursuit divorced from the spirit and soul of who she is on the inside—characterized by a dislike of the self, a hatred of the body, and an obsession over what other people think. Consider my story, which took place during my freshman year in college.

### Chasing Control

I was obsessed with needing to feel in control of my life and my body. But in my pursuit of control, I lost control. Early in my second semester, I was still wrestling with finding my identity and my place within this college, located about six hours away from the small town where I had grown up. In early spring, I started hanging out with a group of senior guys who actually introduced more fun into my life than I had ever experienced. For the first time I actually began to feel that I belonged in college. And I started really liking one of the guys.

It was one of the first warm days of the year, and I was wearing shorts. This guy, for whom I had really started to care, placed his hand on my leg and wiggled it back and forth and said, "You better be careful. It looks like the freshman fifteen are catching up with you." I can recall where we were sitting, what I had on, and the shame I felt come over me. I was so embarrassed.

I quickly became fixated on my thighs. The way it jiggled back and forth under his hand was disgusting to me. Soon I found my entire body was disgusting to me. Clearly my body was not to be trusted. It had betrayed me. Now it needed to be disciplined and controlled. My body became my enemy.

To keep my body under control, I put myself on a "simple diet." (Many years later in my work with the Eating Disorders Coalition of Tennessee I would hear this phrase repeated often

The Perfect Chase

by women and men just like me who found themselves amidst the hell and destruction of an eating disorder after starting just a "simple diet.") I began restricting my food intake, not just how much food I ate but what kinds of food I ate. I had a rigid list of "good" foods and "bad" foods, and I ate only from the good foods list. I also started to exercise daily. I had read in some magazine article about the best workout for weight loss, and I religiously followed the details of the described workout everyday. I allowed myself only that activity for exercise—no intramural fun or other group athletic events—and I would complete the prescribed exercise regimen obsessively. I would never take a day off or allow for exercise substitutions. I might do additional exercises, but I would insist on completing my routine exercises as well. Missing a day was not an option.

My life became consumed with thoughts about my weight, good foods, bad foods, mealtimes, burning calories, avoiding food, and soon avoiding people. My obsession to control my body quickly grew out of control. By the end of the first semester of my sophomore year, it had grown increasingly difficult to concentrate on my class work because my brain and body were starving. I locked myself in broom closets and closed myself off in library carrels just to be alone. I needed the little energy I still could muster to survive and couldn't risk expending it in social relationships. I lost weight and lost myself. My grades declined drastically and so did my will to live. My extreme fixation on body control spun out of control. The all or nothing thinking became a mental prison and a living hell. As my weight continued to drop, I came close to death.

> My obsession to control my body quickly grew out of control.

### The Return Home

It took me a long time and a lot of therapy to break out of that hell and return home from this distant country. A lot longer, I think, than it took the prodigal to come to his senses. Known to be the toughest psychiatric illnesses to treat, recovery from an eating disorder takes an average of seven years. One of the bigger hurdles to get over in eating disorder recovery is coming to terms with the body and accepting ourselves for who we are on the outside and inside. It means having a good life—feeling good and taking care of ourselves—no matter what size we are, instead of just focusing on losing weight. Body acceptance is about saying "NO!" to twisted images of beauty and our cultural obsession with thinness and discrimination based on body size, and about celebrating the beauty of diverse body sizes. People who choose body acceptance can still care about their health and overall fitness, but they choose to stop wasting time with obsessive diets and exercise and make the intentional decision to live their life to the fullest!

Cultivating an internal home of body acceptance is difficult because the subtleties of body hatred are so pervasive in this culture. One can hear girls as young as four years of age speaking negatively about their own thighs, stomach, arms, calves, noses, and ears. We learn early on—girls especially—to dislike what we see, or at least to be critical of it. Sadly, these young children are not articulating genuine sentiment. Rather, they are mirroring behavior they witness all around them. From television commercials to the kitchen table, we are hit from every direction with messages of shaping up and sliming down.

I had a mother break down in my office once out of concern that her thirteen-year-old daughter might be bulimic. The mother was mystified, how could this have happened? Heartbroken over her daughter's constant body put-downs, she opened up to me. "The other morning she was going on and on about how fat her bottom looked. I finally had it. I told her she was NOT fat and that I would show her fat. I took off my jeans and grabbed the fat on my own thighs and said THIS is fat! This is disgusting fat! You, my dear, are NOT fat!" In a sincere and desperate attempt to help her daughter trade in her body disdain for something a bit more loving, the mother put her own body down. Unlike mathematics, two negatives do not make a positive. Putting our own body down in an attempt to help another feel great about his or her body only leaves two individuals bereft of body confidence and acceptance.

Fear is at the core of negative body image. It is fear of not living up to this ideal of perfection that is thrown our way a thousand times a day. Because we cannot live up to this artificially created ideal, we erroneously believe we are not enough—not worthy of friendships, not worthy of intimacy, just not worthy. This feeling of emptiness drives us to destructive life choices. Even if it doesn't materialize into a full-blown eating disorder, our lives are too often compromised by a diseased and distorted understanding of ourselves.

Life is hard and much of it is largely out of our control. So it's alluring to devise a checklist that provides structure and control to the chaos all around us. Living your life in black and white is sometimes easier. With a checklist of dos and don'ts, we can convince ourselves we are granted a special dispensation from life's asymmetry. Perhaps this is the lure of a new diet or plastic surgery or a relentlessly unforgiving workout regimen. These things keep us distracted from the messiness of life. They help tie up life's loose ends. But what is life if not loose ends? Life is scarred and flawless, broken yet whole.

The path of seeking is more circular than linear, and embracing the questions only leads to more questions. In the process of living into the questions and in the uncertainty and the chaos, a real celebration can occur. Notice the endless shades of color found in creation, the unique shape of each individual eye, mouth, and nose, the different ways children laugh, and the many ways we experience silence. Take off your shoes and allow your bare feet to touch the earth. Explore the beautiful gift of your sexuality. Pay attention. Make the decision to reject the fear and ignorance that too often keeps us from exploring and discovering a greater awareness of the Divine Spirit that dwells in each of us. Abandon the checklists, and like the prodigal, return home.

### Connectedness and the *Imago Dei*

Ultimately life is about connectedness: connections between our bodies and our souls, connections between people in a variety of relationships, and connections between humans and animals and the ecosystem. Maybe God is connectedness. Perhaps God is the oneness that connects all of us to each other and to everything else. Made in the image of God, we are connected; and when we embrace our connection to all that is around us, we are able to escape the imprisonment of a warped view of the body and to break into a full expanse of our divinity.

If we embrace this idea that we are all one and that all of life is connected, then we also must realize that we must be responsible and accountable to ourselves and to our neighbors. In this sense, connectedness animates a perfect chase that prompts us to pursue that which is life-sustaining and affirming in ourselves and others. Perhaps in opening ourselves up to the questions, embracing unconditional compassion and the theological tenet that we are all connected, and thus standing accountable to our neighbor, we can move into a more healthy relationship with our self and perhaps realize more clearly what Matthew's gospel means when it says, "Be perfect, therefore, as [God] is perfect." (Mt. 5:48)

As Christians, belief that we are made in the image of God holds a certain power to reframe our understanding and refuel our commitment to community. But before moving far down the path to reimaging God, we must expand the metaphors used in reference to the Divine. The use of female imagery when referring to God has the potential to curb the cultural onslaught of body hatred among women and girls. Such simple yet profound change may encourage the belief in girls that they are fearfully and wonderfully made indeed.

As Christians we believe that we are made in the image of God.

The call to the church then is to risk moving beyond male-exclusive language for God and to include feminine terms for the Divine, not just for those special sermons and occasions, but throughout our worship and everyday. We must speak out! From the pulpit and in the workplace, during Sunday School and happy hour, Bible studies and book club, we must address the normalized body hatred present in our culture and take a stand.

We must be more vigilant in our use of language. In conversation, refuse to accept put-downs and unkind remarks made by others and be aware of the spoken (and unspoken) remarks we too casually make about ourselves. Comments made "in jest" teach others to be overly concerned about externals and critical of their own bodies. Speak kindly and lovingly about your own body. Verbalize the amazing ways your body shows up for you each day. Never criticize another's appearance and be conscious of objectifying. The objectification of both women and men scars all creation. It's a violation that keeps us disconnected from each other and imprisoned in harsh and critical self-judgment.

Rather, praise others for who they are, not how they look. And don't diet. Ever. Diets do not work and send unrealistic messages about quick-fix solutions. Rather than diet, observe a balanced yet flexible routine of nutritious eating and fitness-promoting exercise. Whether you're out with the girls for sushi or Wednesday evening fellowship, during shared meals together avoid comments about what you or someone else is eating and how much. No food is good or bad. Be a conduit of change in the way you recognize and honor the image of God that connects you to all others. And by all means, talk about eating disorders. Identify resources for your congregations and communities and be informed.

Ultimately, we are all connected. We are all accountable to the twelve-year-old girl dying to be thin, the twentysomething who wears a size twenty-something, the middle-aged gay man desperate to be accepted for who he is, and you. If we do not realize that our language and our actions have consequences, then who will? If we do not decide to embody daily the love and oneness of God, then who will? If we fail to work for personal and cultural transformation that will support and encourage all of us seeking to understand our bodies in relation to the *imago Dei*, then who will? And if we cannot see that those in our midst are desperately in need of love and support as they journey toward physical and spiritual health and wholeness, then who does have the eyes to see? If we, who claim to have faith in the One who connects and catches us in the unity of that perfect chase, cannot accept our bodies, be responsible to the world around us and all its inhabitants, and create healthy and balanced relationships with food and exercise and all those external markers of beauty and success, then we really must ask ourselves one of the hardest questions of them all: Why have any faith at all?

## Additional Resources

*Body Positive: Boosting Body Image at Any Weight.* www.
bodypositive.com

BodyImageHealth.org. www.bodyimagehealth.org

Maine, Margo, and Joe Kelly. *The Body Myth: Adult Women and the Pressure to Be Perfect.* Hoboken, N.J.: John Wiley & Sons, 2005.

Martin, Courtney. *Perfect Girls, Starving Daughters: The Frightening New Normalcy of Hating Your Body.* New York: Free Press, 2007.

Paulsell, Stephanie. *Honoring the Body: Meditations on a Christian Practice.* San Francisco: Jossey-Bass, 2002.

# Questions \ for Discussion and Contemplation

1 Is there a time in your life when you've experienced an extreme dissatisfaction with your own body? Can you identify cultural or familial markers that encouraged this dissatisfaction?

2 Yoder believes that our language helps to form our self-awareness. Do you believe that we can alter negative body image by choosing to speak of God in terms other than the masculine? Why or why not?

3 If Christians believe that we are each one a child of God and part of the body of Christ, then we must imagine ourselves responsible to each other for affirming and living out this premise. In what ways have you witnessed this responsibility in terms of body image in your faith community?

4 By using the parable of the prodigal son as a metaphor for the way in which we strive to distance ourselves from our bodies, Yoder posits a biblical framework through which to understand this process. Have you imagined yourself far from home, displaced from your body? How did you find your way home?

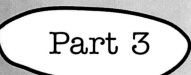

# In Vitro Fertilization

## The Intersection of Fear and Wonder

Chapter 8

Psalm 139 exalts the miracle that God has knit us together in our mother's wombs—that we have all been "fearfully and wonderfully made." I have always embraced this image of our creation for its implication that God, who often seems separated from humanity by chasms of mystery, is actually personally involved in the minutia of reproduction. But my husband and I discovered a whole new depth of meaning in this Psalm as our three-year struggle with infertility ushered us into the unknown world of in vitro fertilization (IVF). The emotional and financial risks we took introduced us to a particular brand of fear we had never before experienced. The IVF process, from the arrival of countless syringes and vials from the mail-order pharmacy to the photo taken of our child when he was just a five-day-old blastocyst, incited in us an unparalleled sense of wonder.

I wish I could say that our decision to make use of reproductive technology was the product of impressive and superhuman levels of emotional and theological clarity. After all, I had invested in my mental health many hours spent in introspection and therapy, and my husband and I had invested in my theological education with four years of compromise and study. However, I found infertility to be one of life's great levelers. I reacted to the monthly reminders of failure, the throng of pregnant women in my community, and a miscarriage due to a tubal pregnancy with the same disappointment, jealousy, self-pity, and questions for God that characterize many infertile women's experiences. It is not that my mental health and faith in God did not come through for me. They did. But they were not the shortcut around the nitty-gritty suffering and doubt that I was hoping for. In the end, the only healthy and faithful way for my husband and me to arrive at a decision about whether or not to see our local fertility specialist was to cling to one another as we braved an abysmal wilderness of heartache.

From this wilderness came the two embarrassingly mundane events that laid the foundation for our life-changing plunge into fear and wonder. The first was what felt to us like the five millionth time we heard the good news that a friend, who did not even want to be pregnant, was expecting a baby and hating every minute of her first-trimester ills. This launched me into the height of what I called "mourning sickness," an all-consuming grief that eclipsed much of my natural compassion and goodwill toward others.

The second was a dialogue that was part of a *West Wing* episode my husband and I watched together. (We had taken to numbing our sorrows with mass quantities of nightly television.) In this episode, President Bartlett is under pressure to decide whether or not to exert his power to stop the execution of a man on death row. He fears he would be playing God by doing so, and he hears advice from a colleague's rabbi as well as a Quaker political advisor. Still undecided, the president meets with his priest at the eleventh hour, and the priest tells Bartlett a familiar theological joke.

In this joke, a man, who lives by a river, is warned that a flood is coming. Though he hears a radio report urging him to evacuate, he resolves to stay, with the logic that God will save him. When the flood waters rise, the man retreats to his roof where he spots a boat. The boat driver offers to paddle the man to safety, but the man refuses, again reasoning that God will save him. Finally, a helicopter hovers above him, and the pilot offers to airlift the man to dry land. The man declines again, assuming that God will save him. The man is swept away to his death by the flood, and when he reaches the pearly gates, he asks God why God did not prevent such a terrible thing from happening to him. God replies, "I sent you a radio report, a helicopter, and a guy in a rowboat. What the hell are you doing here?"

At episode's end, my husband and I looked at each other and asked, "What the hell are we doing here?" We had the resources to invest in reproductive technology and a reputable fertility doctor in town. Our long-standing fears that allowing science to help us get pregnant would constitute playing God were fading in light of the gifts of human intellect and free will. Only then did my theology, honed in divinity school and so attractive in theory, make its way clumsily down to my decisions about reproductive technology. I made the call to the fertility specialist the next day.

Over the years that we failed to conceive and sustain a viable pregnancy, our house was inundated with a passel of unwanted roommates—a range of emotions including despair, disappointment, and all of their needy friends. Yet we were still unprepared for the newcomer who would join us as a result of our visit to the fertility specialist. Fear made its way into our house with an alarming quickness. Conversations with our new doctor made clear that our best option was not the minor procedure we had been hoping for. We learned that IVF would be our best option, an option we had previously been too afraid to seriously consider. IVF would call for me, a needlephobe, to endure daily injections for over two months. Another fear factor was that IVF had always been a sort of safety net for my husband and me. We thought of it only as something we could do if we got really desperate. Going with our unthinkable backup plan felt much like free falling. But the most significant fear came to us as a result of the risk we would be taking. The success rate of IVF for women my age was a mere 61 percent, and the rate of miscarriage brings that statistic down to 57 percent.[1] The fact that one cycle of IVF costs about half as much as a brand new Honda Accord is not something to be taken lightly. But the prevailing terror for me came from the emotional risk involved with the procedure. Could I stand to put such an expansive portion of my hope on the line? How would I put myself back together if IVF did not work for us? How would we put back our marriage? Even as we signed the necessary papers and paid our deposit, I was unsure.

Over the next few months, I learned how to give myself injections. I reported to the doctor's office several times a week for blood work and tests. My husband also endured his share of blood work and tests, and he learned to give me other necessary injections. We both enlarged our vocabularies with phrases such as *uterine lining*, *gonadotropin*, *motility*, and *follicles*. I also reported to a surgery center for my retrieval, a surprisingly painless procedure wherein some twenty plus eggs were extracted from my ovaries. But something else happened during those months that helped me manage my fear: I changed the way I prayed to God.

Not since I was a small child had I prayed to God for specific things. My prayers were always simply for God's will to be done. After all, who am I to determine the way the world should work? Perhaps my prayer life formed this way because my faith grew from strong Presbyterian soil, wherein John Calvin's doctrine of predestination still influences and complicates things. Or perhaps this habit came about as a result of my honest doubt, something I believe is a necessary companion to strong, authentic faith. Either way, I surprised myself by my newfound urge to ask God for specific things. I prayed that I would respond well to the injections, that the IVF would work, that my fear would subside, that my husband and I would continue to be open with each other about our emotions. Once I was pregnant, I begged God daily that the baby remained healthy.

Approaching God opened me up to the sense that God was with me in my most intimate and fragile state.

I cannot pretend to know how and why prayer works or what kind of God is able to be present in so many lives at once. All I know is that my new way of praying helped. It would have helped even if the IVF had not worked or if our pregnancy had ended in miscarriage. My new way of approaching God opened me up to the sense that God was with me in my most intimate and fragile state. I was then able to fully embrace what I have been preaching ever since my ordination: God never promised that we would not suffer. But God did promise that we would never suffer alone.

My prayer life was not the only thing that tempered our IVF-induced fear. Thanks to the mix of modern technology and the intricate order of creation that the procedure revealed, wonder took up residence in our home as well. After over twenty eggs were retrieved from my ovaries, each one had a date with handsome young sperm, carefully washed and spun in preparation for the big day. My husband and I received a phone call on the afternoon of the retrieval from an embryologist, who reported that seventeen of my eggs had fertilized normally. For the next three days, we eagerly anticipated our customary call from the folks in the lab, who would explain to us in great detail how many of our embryos were still in the running and how each of them ranked according to several criteria. We were told that our little petri dish crew was viable enough to remain in their makeshift home for five days, thus allowing them to become blastocysts before entering my body.

Five days from the retrieval, my husband and I returned to the surgery center for another surprisingly painless procedure wherein the only two embryos fit enough to survive the IVF process were carefully placed inside my uterus. We left the surgery center that day with an empty plastic petri dish, the aforementioned picture of the blastocysts that had formerly inhabited it, and a tentative hope that our road to parenthood had officially begun. The inception of life is always full of wonder. But the IVF process made us firsthand witnesses to the inner workings of a miracle.

I spent the following three days on bed rest to allow the embryos the optimum opportunity to implant in my uterus. This time in bed, along with the eleven days until I was to return to the doctor for a pregnancy test, were excruciating. Friends who had preceded my husband and me on this IVF road had accurately warned us that this two-week waiting period would be the hardest stretch. Fear and wonder fought

In Vitro Fertilization

constantly for my attention, and each got equal time. In one moment I would calculate when and how we might do a second IVF procedure if this one had failed. In the next, I would picture myself with twins and brainstorm about what their names might be.

The pregnancy test revealed I was pregnant, and a second test two days later revealed that my hormone levels were doubling properly. About a month later my husband and I returned for our first ultrasound, where we saw our healthy baby's heartbeat for the first time. The wonder continued as we were privy to countless ultrasounds reserved only for IVF and high-risk pregnancies. We returned with pictures of our baby at eight weeks, ten weeks, twelve weeks, and fourteen weeks, and we toted these early documents of progress everywhere so others could experience the wonder with us.

IVF allowed my husband and me to be more fully present in the fear and wonder that is part of a child's entrance into the world. But my time in and around the fertility clinic also revealed that the fear and wonder of other couples is often even more intense than that of my husband and me. Because we had only two embryos left on the day of the transfer and were open to having twins, we did not have to make the difficult decisions many couples make about how many embryos to transfer or what to do with remaining embryos. I also saw couples in the waiting room whose greatest fears had come true. The procedures were not working on them, or their successful pregnancies had ended prematurely. In contrast, I rode the elevator up to the office one day with a woman who was my age and had been undergoing IVF cycles for four years. We were both returning to the clinic for follow-up blood work after our initial positive pregnancy tests. Never before had she received a positive reward for the great risks she and her husband had been taking. And never before had I seen the kind of wonder that inhabited her that day. My husband and I felt cursed during our years of infertility that gave way to an existence filled with syringes, minor surgeries, and shot schedules. But in the end, we cannot help but feel lucky. IVF worked for us on the first try. Not all IVF journeys end in the kind of immeasurable gratitude that marks our current life.

In August of 2006, our healthy baby boy was born. He is now a spirited toddler with wild, blond, curly hair and a boundless affection for other people and life. My husband and I initially shared our infertility struggles and IVF experiences with friends and family because we desperately needed their support. The fact that we live in a world where IVF is increasingly common and decreasingly stigmatized has allowed us to remain candid about the way our little boy came into the world without significantly jeopardizing his future peer relationships. Fifteen years ago, such truth telling would not have been an option.

My hope is that our son will eventually regard his particular creation story as a source for his already fierce sense of wonder, an appreciation for how fragile and resilient life is from the beginning, and the knowledge that his father and I loved him for years before he was ever even born. For me, this is the story of the greatest lesson I have encountered so far about who I am and who God is. My willingness to face my fears for the sake of my child has given me a new perspective on the sacrifices God has made in order to know us. And finally, because my little boy continues to delight me with wonder by the very fact of his existence, I now know deep down in my bones that none of us has to achieve perfection to merit God's love. God delights in us simply because we are. As it turns out, the phrase we say during baptism is true: We love because God first loved us.

*God delights in us simply because we are.*

## Additional Resources

Geis, Sally B., and Donald E. Messer, eds. *The Befuddled Stork: Helping Persons of Faith Debate Beginning of Life Issues.* Nashville: Abingdon Press, 2000.

Peters, Ted. *For the Love of Children: Genetic Technology and the Future of the Family.* Louisville: Westminster John Knox Press, 1996.

Rae, Scott. *Brave New Families: Biblical Ethics and Reproductive Technologies.* Grand Rapids: Baker, 1996.

In Vitro Fertilization

# Questions \ for Discussion and Contemplation

1 Share your own birth story. When were you born? Where? Who are you named after and what does that mean to you?

2 Beasley Cates writes, "And finally, because my little boy continues to delight me with wonder by the very fact of his existence, I now know deep down in my bones that none of us has to achieve perfection to merit God's love." When have you experienced this sort of love, and did it help lead you to this realization as well? Why or why not?

3 Recently, techniques such as IVF have become increasingly common, yet people often still refer to this as "playing God." Do you believe Christianity speaks to this issue at all? If so, what does it have to say?

4 Read Psalm 139. Beasley Cates claims that this psalm affirms her belief that God is intricately involved in the most specific aspects of conception. Do you understand and agree or disagree with her interpretation? How else might this psalm be read?

## "A Wild Ass at Home in the Wilderness"
### Fidelity and the Life of Faith in a Hypersexualized, Consumer-driven Culture

Chapter 9

*You shall not commit adultery." But I say to you that everyone who looks at a woman with lust has already committed adultery with her in his heart.* • Mt. 5:27–28

*But you said, 'It is hopeless, for I have loved strangers, and after them I will go.'* • Jer. 2:25

Jesus concludes the above, "you have heard it said...but I say to you" revision of the seventh commandment in Matthew with a freakish image of tearing out your eye and throwing it away if it causes you to sin, "for it is better for you to lose one of your members than for your whole body to be thrown into hell." This is a harsh and violent idea. It sounds more like Rob Zombie than gentle Jesus, meek and mild. (Of course, Jesus *isn't* meek and mild, and Rob Zombie *was* the bike messenger on *Pee-Wee's Playhouse*, so I guess you can't always trust first impressions.) But still, the idea of removing your own eyeball in some violent way (common English translations include the words "gouge" (NIV) "poke" (TEV) and my personal favorite from the King James Version, "pluck"[1]) and then throwing it in the trash seems like some draconian self punishment for ogling the Victoria Secret catalogue.

Before I laugh and point at Jesus for his quaint and simplistic ideas about sexuality and purity that only an idealistic young man who is still single at age thirty could possibly cook up, I must admit this truth: Something about eyeing others with lust is thoroughly anti-relationship. And in the Christian view of reality, anti-relationship is anti-God. Some switch is pulled in my mind when I look at another person and think, in the eloquent words of Borat, "Wow-wow-wee-waa!" My eyes are drawn away from the eyes, the windows of the soul, of the other, and they feast on the hourglass flesh of the middle torso. The woman becomes an object.

*anti-relationship is anti-God*

I think Eugene Peterson brings things into two-eyed, three-dimensional perspective when he translates the whole thing like this:

> You know the next commandment pretty well, too: 'Don't go to bed with another's spouse.' But don't think you've preserved your virtue simply by staying out of bed. Your heart can be corrupted by lust even quicker than your body. Those leering looks you think nobody notices—they also corrupt. Let's not pretend this is easier than it really is. If you want to live a morally pure life, here's what you have to do: You have to blind your right eye the moment you catch it in a lustful leer. You have to choose to live one-eyed or else be dumped on a moral trash pile.[2]

I like Peterson's version of that passage because it doesn't use any language that makes me remember putting my hand in the bowl of peeled grapes through a curtain labeled "fresh eyeballs" at the Happy Hollow Elementary spook-house in fourth grade, and because it uses the word "corrupt" in the description of what happens when we look at others with the intention of having sex with them. The word "corrupt" here implies that Jesus speaks of the objectification of another, and Jesus knew that objectification of other people leads to using them. And using others leads to hating them.

Objectifying others corrupts the human to human, the human to God, and the human to creation relationships for which we believe God created us. When God creates Eve in the story at the beginning of Genesis, Adam speaks his first words in poetry about her,

> "This is now bone of my bones
> and flesh of my flesh;
> she shall be called 'woman,'
> for she was taken out of man." • Gen. 2:23, NIV

Relationship is as basic to us as speech. The process of naming her *woman* is not a signifier of dominance. Instead, naming the woman is a dynamic element of the creative process and connotes discernment of the relationship rather than dominance or objectification. One main point of the Adam and Eve story is that a primary ingredient in humanity (besides dirt) is relationship.

Relationship is also basic to God in scripture. In the garden of Eden, God walks around and interacts with humans personally. God "called to the man, and said to him 'Where are you?'" (Gen. 3:9), and the humans hide for shame of their nakedness when they hear God's approaching footsteps. Christians believe that the most explicit act of God's desire for relationship with humanity is God's incarnation in the person of Jesus Christ of Nazareth: a boy who was born to a family, and a man who gathered friends and disciples and healed strangers.

Classical orthodox theology insists that the dynamic relationship we perceive in the Trinity is an ultimate reality of God. God is a relational Trinity within the Godhead, not just an appearance of three from the outside. "This relationship at the core of God is described in the classical doctrines of the Trinity as "indivisibly One, eternally and mutually dwelling in one another."[3] Isn't that a beautiful description? When I read "mutual dwelling in one another," in my mind I see a beautiful endless spiral. Gregory of Nazianzus, a fourth-century church father, used the Greek term *perichoresis*, which means "circuition, going around," to describe the dynamic reality of the Trinity. John of Damascus, in the eighth century, more fully developed the doctrine of *perichoresis* and used it especially to convey what in English we call "envelopment."

In Eastern Christianity, perichoresis is associated with unification with the Godhead upon sanctification. Redeemed humanity is drawn into the circulation of divine love and thus participates in the coinherence of the Divine Persons, referring to texts such as John 17:22–23, 26:

> The glory that you have given me I have given them, so that they may be one, as we are one, I in them and you in me, that they may become completely one, so that the world may know that you have sent me and have loved them even as you have loved me...that the love with which you have loved me may be in them, and I in them.

Interestingly enough, if you replace the omega with its long "o" sound in the word *perichoresis*, with an omicron, a short "o" sound, you have the Greek word for "dance." Isn't that beautiful? God's very being is not far removed from the idea of an endless, mutual dance, and God is inviting us to be a part of the dance. The prophets write poetically about how God responds to humanity when the invitation to dance is rejected or when we dance with others. To condense the theme of much of the marital imagery in the prophets with a truly junior-high metaphor: the invitation to dance with the finest girl in the ninth grade isn't heard because we are too busy frenching the seventh grade sluts in the dark corners of the celestial junior high gym.

If you think that sounds harsh or insensitive, take note that the title to this chapter refers to Jeremiah's characterization of Israel "playing the whore" and going after other gods, like the Baals.

> How can you say, 'I am not defiled,
>     I have not gone after the Baals'?
> Look at your way in the valley;
>     know what you have done—
> a restive young camel interlacing her tracks,
>     a wild ass at home in the wilderness,

in her heat sniffing the wind!
> Who can restrain her lust?

None who seek her need weary themselves;
> in her month they will find her. • Jer. 2:23-24

The language and imagery of Israel committing infidelity on God is a dominant one in the prophets. It provides the major template for the book of Hosea, which, because of the passionate verbosity of the Divine haranguing in Hebrew, is one of the most appalling and disturbing and at the same time beautiful books of the Bible. You know those arguments you sometimes have with those you love the most that get you so frustrated you can barely think, much less speak, straight? God can relate, as we see in Hosea.

Hosea's focus on the subject of God's relationship with an adulterous Israel is the most comprehensive and first prophetic treatment of the topic in the Bible, but the same subject can be seen in Isaiah, Jeremiah, Ezekiel, Micah, and elsewhere. The image of a jilted spouse, angry and hurt over the other's infidelity, is found so often in scripture because humans have a deep-seated inclination toward sexual and spiritual dissatisfaction and wandering. This is why marriage is a covenant, which lifts both participants into a way of being that is not quite natural, or fallen. The prophets point to a God who is jealously passionate about our fidelity. God expects monogamy.

I've always been interested to hear about sexual monogamy in the animal kingdom. It is found more often in the bird kingdom than in the mammalian. Eagles and swans take on one partner for life, and sometimes that is true with humans too. Margaret Mead, the cultural anthropologist, said "monogamy is the most difficult of all marital arrangements."[4] Perhaps that is why so few species actually engage in it.

The Bible itself doesn't provide the framework for a monogamous marriage. Instead, marriage in the majority of cases in scripture refers to polygamy, with one man and several women. In this day and age, when untold numbers of marriages suffer from the infidelity of a spouse, are we being too hard on ourselves expecting fidelity in monogamy if we

"A Wild Ass at Home in the Wilderness"

weren't engineered to be one-to-one pairs? David Barash and spouse/coauthor Judith Eve Lipton argue in their book *The Myth of Monogamy* that the threat to "family values," though usually pinned on the secular, leftist, scientistic, NPR–listening, purple-triangle Teletubbies, is actually from a more ominous source: biology. Good news for those who don't subscribe philosophically (or practically) to monogamy. Maybe humans are biologically wired for a more freewheeling existence. Of course, humans are also rare among the mammalian world in that we (some of us) are fortunate enough to have male participation in child rearing. This is another trait we share with the birds.

However we define marriage, clearly God intends for us to live within the bounds of the covenant that we take in marriage, whether that be with one or two or three or more spouses. Sure, we can make excuses for ourselves: "I'm not supposed to want to remain faithful to my wife. I'm supposed to want to spread my seed." If monogamy is so counter to our existence, then why should we celebrate it?

> However we define marriage, clearly God intends for us to live within the bounds of that covenant.

Fidelity is first of all a celebration of the Divine breath God gave us that lifts us above our animal existence. Animals, for the most part, aren't cognizant of the feelings of others. We have that ability (or we usually do) because God endows us with the divine quality of empathy. We feel and know that our actions cause feelings in others. I know that my wife would experience great pain and anger if I were to cheat on her. Animals aren't endowed with this foresight (and they might not be endowed with the depth of anger, pain, and resentment caused by infidelity, or anything else for that matter, that our large brains tend to produce.) So looking to the animal kingdom for an excuse for infidelity is not a great direction. Perhaps, as a signature of the incompleteness of the process of our biological evolution, our animal desire to find as many sex partners as possible to guarantee diversity and health hasn't equalized with the tremendous growth in our mental and emotional abilities. But that is the price of being human. That is the difficulty with which we must strive. The

Christian conundrum is between being a slave to the desires that push us or to the vision of a "new heaven and earth" that pulls us. As Wesleyan theology says, God has given us grace and responsibility: grace to experience the joy of covenant and acceptance, and responsibility to know the sorrow caused by rejection and infidelity.

Fidelity in marriage is the honoring of a covenant. Love, as C. S. Lewis said, is an act of will. Being "in love" is a feeling that changes. Practicing fidelity to the marriage covenant involves being defined in relationship by our will rather than our feelings. This may be an unpopular statement in a culture and time when a premium is paid to feelings, but life and religious faith are about more than feelings. In *Mere Christianity*, C. S. Lewis writes that the promise of covenant made in a public marriage ceremony is made while one is in love, but must last even if the feeling of being "in love" wears off. Of course, feeling "in love" is not a negative thing. It gives us courage and generosity, and broadens our perspective beyond ourselves. But the feeling of "being in love" is incomplete. Lewis relies on another aspect of love that is the engine of fidelity in marriage.

Rob Bell distinguishes the different aspects of love in the Hebrew poetry of the Song of Solomon as *ahava*, or the deep aspect of love expressed in commitment, and *dod*, which is the excitement of erotic love. Both, as well as *raya*, which is the companionship and friendship aspect of love, are involved in relationship.[5] C. S. Lewis places the weight of fidelity in relationship on the *ahava* aspect of love, which he calls, "a quieter" kind of love. He also points out (quite amusingly in his dry fashion of wit) that it is a gift to us to not experience the ecstasy of being "in love" for the duration of our lives, because being in love is exhausting, and we'd miss out on a lot of meals and sleep. Yet this is an area where the values and philosophy of our culture usually reign supreme over the values and philosophy of our faith. Being "in love" is defined for us by the movies, by the commercials, and by television as the par excellence of human existence.

The trump card in our appreciation of the love between two people is that romantic love called *dod*: "Bill and Carol are so sweet. They've been married for nineteen years and they are just so in love." If we don't experience that romance in our relationship, if we don't feel "in love" with our spouse, then we certainly look with wistfulness at those relationships where that "in love" spark is so evident and think to ourselves, "Well, what's wrong with me?" Or perhaps more truthfully, "What's wrong with my spouse?" Then, because we are quite thoroughly shaped by the consumerism that drives this fascination with romantic love, we probably start imagining someone we really could see ourselves being "in love" with again. We might even strike out in pursuit of rekindling that feeling. We want a new one. We want to "get someone" who makes us feel appreciated, interesting, and vigorous, because in the end, my life is about the satisfaction of my wants, my needs, and my feelings.[6]

We live in a culture where the greatest risk of idolatry is found in self-worship. Consumerism backs us into the dark corner of self-worship by making us believe what we have isn't good enough. We become inwardly focused, trying to acquire more and better things that will give us enhanced self-worth. We spend so much time chasing what we don't have that we forget to cultivate what we've already been given. It's a disease of our culture that has been called "affluenza." And as C. S. Lewis points out, the life of abandoning a committed relationship and chasing the next thrill inevitably leads to disillusionment and dissatisfaction.

Because we live in relationship with God too, is it any surprise that these same dynamics apply there as well? We might think of *dod* as those ecstatic moments where we feel the power and presence of God. They might be experienced as a sense of connectedness or transcendence. Some mystics, such as Teresa of Avila, Francis of Assisi, and Rumi have spoken of that ecstatic experience having the properties of sensuality and eroticism. Rumi wrote about God in a style in the thirteenth century that is admired by couples today for its romance and electricity. Even Thomas Aquinas, known more for his categorization and institution of doctrine than his ecstatic poetry, penned quite a few romantic poems to God.[7] These experiences are those moments when we feel "in love" with or completely accepted by God.

*Consumerism drives our fascination with romantic love.*

But we don't live every moment in a state of ecstatic enlightenment. If we expect that of our spiritual relationship with God, then we are likely to be filled with despair and disillusionment. The "quieter love" sustains the in-between times. Another way to think of this quieter love is faith, and the expression of this faith is faithfulness, fidelity translated quite literally from its Latin roots. Faith is the "assurance of things hoped for, and the conviction of things unseen," as Hebrews 11:1 puts it. This less glamorous kind of love is not only the engine of marriage; it is also the engine of a relationship with God. This is why so much of the Bible is about covenant. A covenant binds people together and lifts us up to a higher plane of relationship. It lifts us out of the bog of endless self-gratification. It carries us through times of wilderness. It is forged in the wilderness, as the example of the law being given at Mt. Sinai in the book of Exodus reveals.

When I was a youth minister, I took a group of youth to Kansas City from Bartlesville, Oklahoma, in our new church bus. On our return, the weather through Kansas was getting nasty. Tornados were touching down west of us, but I knew we could get out of the path of the tornados if we only could get to our southern road. We had no safe places to stop in rural Kansas, so I barged on ahead with the hope that I would be able to keep the kids out of harm's way. The wind caught the shell top van like a sail and blew it around on the road as I white-knuckled the steering wheel. The kids were laughing and carrying on in the back, oblivious to the pit I had in my stomach. My prayer to God was less a petition and more a pissed off demand. "These are your children, God, and I'm all you've got to keep them safe," I prayed, "So I need you to show me you're with me!" Within minutes, a lighting bolt struck a tree that was about a hundred yards outside my driver's window in a pasture right as I was looking at it, and the tree burst into flames. A resounding "coooooool" was mixed with shrieks of fear from the seats behind me. It was as if I had not been riding in the van all along. My mind had been racing with possibilities of all the things that could go wrong. After I witnessed my own "burning bush" though, I had a new sense of confidence in God's presence. The rain didn't let up, the wind still rocked the van, and the wet road continued to slow us down; but now my grip on the wheel relaxed, the blood rushed back into my knuckles, and I was able to feel the road better because I had loosened up enough to actually feel it.

If anything has taught me about fidelity and infidelity in relationship, it has been this experience of a God who responds so convincingly to my prayers, and this same God who seems so blatantly silent the majority of the time—this God who grabs me by the throat, but at other times seems illusive and distant.[8] About nine years have passed since that moment when God's presence was so undeniable and vivid. Most of the time, if I'm paying attention at all, God's presence is in a "still small voice," and not a lightning bolt. In the in-between times, when I'm not speechless and my hair isn't standing up on end, I need a covenant relationship.

> In the in-between times, I need a covenant relationship.

A covenant requires remembrance. This is why the Passover Seder is of central importance to Judaism. This is why wedding anniversaries probably deserve more attention than a nice dinner. How many couples reread marriage vows from time to time? If I weren't speaking them to other people for them to repeat, I probably wouldn't myself. The traditions of our faith utilize our capacity for mentally embedding principles and ideas through repetition and nostalgia. It's an ingenious mechanism that only a God who knows us so well could create. Yet what do couples do at wedding anniversaries? Do we remind ourselves of the covenant to take each other "for better, for worse, for richer, for poorer, in sickness and in health"? No, we give each other stuff. We might go out for a romantic dinner and spend more than we can afford. We fall prey to the cultural expressions of "being in love." We try, at least for one night, not to spoil anything. We try to remind each other of who we were when we were dating: beautiful, gift giving, younger, exuberant. Covenant requires remembrance of what the covenant actually is. It is not "to always feel in love." It is "to love and to cherish, from this day forward."

The ecstatic *dod* can and does occur throughout a person's life, punctuating the quieter valleys of faithfulness and growing in grace with mountaintop experiences that provide a "refueling" along the way. This occurs in both human to human relationships and in human to God relationships. Sometimes we are surprised by a lightning bolt of enlightenment or an unexpected period of passionate romance in an established relationship. These moments of ecstasy can be cultivated by practices of devotion and interest. Cultivation doesn't mean we can force something to grow. It means we nurture and give attention to the season of the present moment. Feelings may cause us to lose interest in our covenanted partner, but the covenant bond should lead us to creatively reinvest ourselves in that partner. That is another facet of the *imago Dei* that we carry within us: creativity. If we have no willingness to get creative with our covenant relationship, we are failing to use all our capacities as carriers of the Divine spark. C. S. Lewis takes Jesus' dictum that a thing will not really live unless it first dies and applies it to the notion of allowing a relationship to mature and follow its own course rather than expecting an endless resuscitation of the thrill of "being in love." That means letting go of the thrill of being in love. When we turn loose of the way our relationship with God or our mate "should be," we let it die so that it can live.

With that difficult saying of Jesus, I return to the original difficult statement. Jesus wants us to be chaste even with our eyeballs and fantasy life. Where does one draw the line? Is it okay to look at *Playboy* but harmful to engage in hardcore pornography on the Internet? (I say "engage in" pornography because it seems unlikely to me that anyone who "looks at" pornography simply looks at it.) Perhaps this is why Jesus warns us about fantasizing in the heart—it dehumanizes the object of our fantasy. When I look at the Victoria Secret catalogue and admire the beautiful bodies, I am not admiring the person, I am admiring the body. It turns a "thou" into a "that."[9] The more I get used to observing the world around me in this way, the more likely I am to come to a cheaper understanding of the life around me (including the life of the spouse to whom I am linked and even my own.)

In a present and a future where technological advancements have made available everything from pornography on the Internet, to virtual visual sex, even to sex with lifelike sex-dolls and humanoid robots,[10] some who are drawn to acting on the thrill of erotic love but not willing to cross the boundary of sex with another person may mistakenly turn to these outlets to relieve the stress of sexual frustration. I say "mistakenly," because, even if the spouse is aware of the other's technological philandering and tacitly approves because of a shared dissatisfaction with the sexual component of the relationship or simply an unwillingness to get in the way of the other blowing off steam, the person engaging in forms of sexual gratification outside the covenant bond is conditioning him or herself for infidelity. One might say, "Well, that's not another person, there's a difference when you have sex with another person." Why is that? Is it that a connection between two living souls brings a disgrace to the maintained connection between two covenanted souls? What if one person doesn't view the prostitute with whom he is having sex with any sense of humanity?

There has been much attention lately on the use of internet pornography among clergy. The cover art of a recent *Christian Century* on the subject of clergy and pornography shows a man sitting at a computer with a shackle around his foot stretching up to the monitor of the computer.[11] That picture contains a thousand words as to why the engagement with pornography and other forms of technologically enhanced sexual gratification are corrosive to relationships and corrupting to the heart. Engaging in these forms of self-gratification is addictive. They engrain the mind with the notion that sex is about the fulfillment of an impulse for physical pleasure instead of the powerful way we nurture a covenant between two people. Because they are so easy to obtain (excepting the $15,000 doll), they not only promote an obsession with sex, they also promote an obsession with a false and empty understanding of sex.

This false and empty understanding of sex pervades our culture. We see it all around. Another metaphor that C. S. Lewis uses to demonstrate our corrupted approach to sexuality is of a striptease where everyone is on the edge of their seats, anxiously awaiting the unveiling of a strip of bacon. Lewis analyzes the possibility that such a show would indicate that the culture where that kind of striptease could be found is starving, and by correlation that our culture is sex starved. Lewis rejects that notion though by pointing out that at no time in history has sex been less costly (because of birth control) or shunned. He doesn't locate our fascination with sex in starvation. He associates it instead with the obsession of gluttony.

I would agree with Lewis that we are gorged on sexuality, but I would make a distinction. Every indication in the current time is that we are gluttons of false and empty sexuality, and starving for nourishing sexuality. We are sexually obese. Because empty and meaningless sexuality fills up our mental space, we are missing the nutrients of nourishing sexuality. Perhaps the recent churchwide campaign in a Texas megachurch promoting sex between spouses for "seven straight days" is a response to this lack of nourishment.[12]

The words of Jesus found in Matthew may be harsh, but they are true. Like all the words of Jesus found in the gospels, they hold tremendous power for us if put into application, if not going so far as to remove my own eye, then at least in the striving to blind ourselves to the cheap and hollow expressions of sexuality all around us and instead to celebrate sexuality for what it is intended.

Fidelity (in thought and in practice) is the rejection of a culture obsessed with sex and objectification. It is a refusal to submit to applying the consumerist mind-set toward humans. When Christianity hasn't been completely enveloped by the culture where it resides, it usually has some aspect of protest against the dehumanization found therein. It has been a powerful voice against racial inequality, slavery, the caste system, violence, and genocide.[13] In the current era, the Christian witness of fidelity also speaks with a powerful voice. Fidelity is an act of protest against the objectification

> Fidelity (in thought and in practice) is the rejection of a culture obsessed with sex and objectification.

of the body and the consumerization of relationship in a hypersexualized, consumer-driven culture. It is a statement that our lives are about more than the gratification of our own wants, needs, and feelings. It is a statement that relationship is a basic ingredient of humanity, and that we should treat each other with the same respect and humility we owe to our God. It is a statement that love is more powerful than the ebb and flow of feelings and emotions, and that we have the capacity to enter into this love, harness it and be the conduits of it. It is the statement that God is love.

## Additional Resources

Bell, Rob. *Sex God: Exploring the Endless Connections between Sexuality and Spirituality.* Grand Rapids: Zondervan, 2007.

Kazantzakis, Nikos. *The Last Temptation of Christ.* New York: Simon and Schuster, 1960.

Lewis, C. S. *Mere Christianity.* New York: MacMillan, 1952.

Ortlund Jr., Raymond C. *Whoredom: God's Unfaithful Wife in Biblical Theology.* Grand Rapids: Eerdmans, 1996.

Rice, Anne. *Christ the Lord: The Road to Cana.* New York: Knopf, 2008.

Yee, Gale. "Hosea." In *The New Interpreter's Bible.* Nashville: Abingdon Press, 2003.

# Questions \ for Discussion and Contemplation

1 Mattox claims that "God's very being is not very far removed from the idea of an endless, mutual dance, and God is inviting us to be a part of the dance." What metaphor would you use to describe your relationship with God and why?

2 "Fidelity is first of all a celebration of the Divine breath God gives us that lifts us above our animal existence." In what ways have you experienced the promise of fidelity? How does that experience impact your relationship to God? How has an experience of infidelity influenced your relationship to God?

3 What examples of culture's fascination with being "in love" can you point to? How does being "in love" differ from practicing love on a daily basis? Do you have a personal experience with this difference?

4 Mattox asserts, "We are sexually obese. Because empty and meaningless sexuality fills up our mental space, we are missing the nutrients of nourishing sexuality" found in fidelity. To what kinds of sexuality might he be referring? Are there times in your life when you've felt "sexually obese"? How has this interfered with your self-identity as a child of God?

# Mustard Seed–Sized Faith

### Isolation and Infertility

**Chapter 10**

On the corner of my desk in my office sits a small glass jar of mustard seeds that my husband gave me for Valentine's Day this year. On the side of the jar is written, "Faith: 2008." This may not seem like a romantic gift, but when I received it my heart swelled with love for this man. The mustard seed is an important symbol for our journey together to be parents.

In the seventeenth chapter of Matthew a man comes seeking Jesus' healing for his epileptic son. The man has already asked the disciples for their healing power for the boy, but they have been unable to help him. Jesus becomes frustrated with the lack of faith of his disciples. After he heals the boy, he responds in frustration to their question about why they could not drive the demon out of the boy as he says, "Because of your little faith. For truly I tell you, if you have faith the size of a mustard seed, you will say to this mountain, 'Move from here to there,' and it will move; and nothing will be impossible for you"(Mt. 17:20).

When your deepest desire in the world is to become a parent, and month after month your attempts to conceive fail, you can easily lose faith just as the disciples did. They could not understand why they were unable to heal the boy; and my husband and I shake our heads and wonder, "Why is this so hard for us?" However, we believe with all of our hearts that with God all things are indeed possible and that some day we will become parents. As for how we will become parents (we do not yet know the answers), we live daily with the uncertainty, the disappointment, and the frustration. I can tell you that some days faith the size of a tiny mustard seed seems almost too much for us to muster up about our situation. I am so grateful that Jesus didn't say that it took a swimming pool full or a Grand Canyon full of faith, but instead required only a tiny mustard seed.

### Our Story

David and I share a story common to many young adults of our current day: we met over the Internet. After moving to rural Tennessee and serving my church for two years, I realized that dating in a small town in the South when you are a female minister is tough. So I took a cue from many of my friends who had success with online dating and joined a service. A friend actually passed me David's profile, and I began the process of getting to know this warm, wonderful, and funny man. Living two hours apart, we saw each other on weekends and fell in love quickly. I introduced him first to my church family, and then to my biological family after a few months of dating. No one was surprised when we were engaged by December after meeting at the end of February. From the beginning, David and I spoke openly about what is most important in our lives, and before we got married we agreed that we were both eager to become parents. Our wedding was a wonderful day when we made sacred vows in front of our friends, families, and church to become a loving family together.

I had some suspicions that I might have trouble conceiving, and after six months of trying to conceive on our own using a digital ovulation monitor (it never indicated that I ovulated in the entire six months), we went to my doctor to begin the infertility journey. After tests that revealed a low sperm count and a possible blocked fallopian tube, along with the complication of an ovulation, we were referred to a fertility center two hours away from our home.

During an intense four months of treatment at the fertility center, we did blood tests, ultrasounds (three to be exact), more semen analysis, and a procedure to see if my fallopian tubes were blocked (neither one was). During this time we attempted but did not complete two different cycles of intrauterine insemination. I was diagnosed with polycystic ovarian syndrome and began medication for that, and I took three cycles of fertility drugs.[1] Each step of the process came with new emotions, including fear, frustration, hopefulness, disappointment, and anger. At the end of the four months we were back to where we started, hearing again that in vitro fertilization would be our best chance for conceiving a biological child.

Too tired, too dismayed, too frustrated, and too full of hormones, I could no longer continue down this road. I asked David one day, "How would you feel if we just put this all on hold for awhile?" Tremendously supportive of my mental health recovery, he encouraged me to give my stress and anxiety about our infertility a vacation. I called the clinic to cancel our next appointment, and we went camping and white-water rafting with some friends.

Taking a break from fertility treatments is where we still stand as I write this. We are still considering both the possibility of in vitro fertilization and adoption. In the meantime we laugh more, we feel less stressed, and we enjoy our marriage more. Being infertile takes a toll on the body, mind, and spirit. Our church is vital to our life as a couple and to us individually; therefore, I want to imagine how the church can be a source of community and support for young adults who experience the isolation of infertility. According to Resolve.org, infertility affects 7.3 million people in the United States each year; that is one in eight couples. This means, whether we acknowledge it or not, that people in churches are experiencing this stress and heartbreak.

### Infertility Struggles in the Bible

In the Bible we encounter all kinds of stories from the lives of God's people. Sometimes we can see ourselves in their stories, and it comforts us to find them vulnerable, emotional, and struggling just as we are. In particular, the stories of three Hebrew women who experienced infertility can speak to fundamental themes the church should address. These women's stories provide an intimate portrait of the consequences of infertility because they lived in a culture where both female identity and economic security revolved around the ability to conceive and bear children.

### Sarai

In the sixteenth chapter of Genesis, we read that Sarai has been unable to have children. In order to fulfill this desire for children, she urges her husband to take her servant Hagar as a wife so that she might bear him children. When Hagar conceives, Sarai has a hard time dealing with the situation; she is bitter and jealous of Hagar. Sarai feels that Hagar is looking down on her and begins to treat Hagar harshly. Hagar flees from Sarai's anger, but hears from one of God's messengers that she will have more descendants and that she needs to go back to her home.

*A jealous Sarai banishes Hagar*

Sarai is still without a child of her own, and in chapters 17 and 18, God makes a covenant with Abram. God promises they will be exceedingly fruitful, and Sarai will bear him a son who will give rise to nations. As a sign of the covenant, Abram is circumcised, and God changes their names to Abraham and Sarah. Can you imagine desiring a child so deeply and being barren for so many years only to be told that you will give birth? I can imagine much disbelief on Sarah's part. The only response to such amazing and mysterious news is Sarah's delightful reaction. When holy visitors come for a visit and tell Abraham that Sarah will have a son, she overhears them and laughs out loud! She and Abraham are too old, they don't even enjoy each others' company sexually anymore. Sarah laughs and says that surely she is too old to have a child. The statement comes from God, "Is anything too wonderful for the Lord?" (Gen. 18:14) When a barren woman is able to conceive after years of heartache, surely one can say that nothing is too wonderful for God! I know many stories of couples who have given up on all fertility treatments and out of the blue they receive a positive pregnancy test. I'm sure many of these couples have laughed as Sarah did and proclaimed, "Is nothing too wonderful for God?"

### Rachel

In the twenty-ninth chapter of Genesis, we encounter another sister in the infertility journey. Rachel is the beloved second wife of Jacob. Rachel is barren, but her sister Leah, Jacob's first wife, gives birth four times. Rachel is jealous of her sister and angry at her husband, and in chapter 30 she finally cries out, "Give me children, or I shall die!" (v. 1) How common these emotions of jealousy, anger, and desperation are to a person experiencing infertility.

Rachel gives her maidservant to her husband, who bears him two children. In the meantime, her sister Leah's servant also bears a second child. Desperate and willing to try anything to have a child, Rachel asks for mandrakes, an ancient fertility treatment that Leah's son brought her. Rachel is willing to do whatever it takes, even give her sister another night with their husband in exchange for this treatment. Leah conceives once again (apparently those mandrakes worked for her!) and gives birth to two more sons and a daughter. Finally, something miraculous happens in verse 22 "Then God remembered Rachel, and God heeded her and opened her womb." At long last, Rachel's pleading prayers are answered in the birth of her son Joseph. What we hear in her story is a sense that while she is infertile, she feels unheard by God. We know in our rational minds that God does not always answer our prayers on our timeline or in just the ways we would like. However, when our prayers for children go unanswered, we can easily feel as if we are not being heard by God. Rachel's story gives us permission to feel many of the emotions that come with infertility: anger, jealousy, and desperation. Some of us on this journey feel as strongly as our sister Rachel when she cries out, "Give me children, or I shall die."

### Hannah

In the Christian Church (Disciples of Christ), we participate in believer's baptism, meaning we do not baptize infants. Many of our congregations offer instead an infant dedication service, presenting a child to God in front of the church family. Each time we have one of these services at our church and I see a new child's parents come before the church and present this child as a gift from God, I think of our sister Hannah.

In the first chapter of Samuel, Hannah, who is one of the two wives of Elkanah, has no children, and Elkanah's other wife has children. Elkanah brings home double portions of his food sacrifice for Hannah, because he loves her and feels sorry that she has no children. This favoritism creates tension at home, and Hannah is still heartbroken and wanting a child. She decides to go to the temple and pray to the Lord on her own behalf. When the priest Eli sees her there praying and crying bitterly, he thinks she is drunk. When she explains herself, Eli tells her to "go in peace," and that God will hear and answer her petition.

Hannah conceives, and when she gives birth to Samuel, she presents him back to the temple in service to God. Hannah knows that this child belongs to God, and that he is an answered prayer. Hannah's frame of mind is helpful for those of us who pray earnestly to become parents. Whether infertile couples conceive while on a break from fertility treatments or through the process of any assisted reproductive methods, whether they adopt or become foster parents, whatever children a couple is blessed with ultimately belong to God. Even though fertility treatments can feel scientific and clinical, surely technology that can give hope to infertile couples—hope that our biblical sisters and brothers never had—is a true miracle. Thus any child who comes to be in the care of parents who have faced infertility has been given by the grace of God. Baby dedications are a wonderful chance to acknowledge to whom a child truly belongs. Hannah prayed earnestly, conceived miraculously, and returned thanks to God for the child entered into her life.

### The Biblical Witness

For those of us still waiting to conceive, the stories of three women who inexplicably conceive might seem discouraging. However, I think looking closely at the lives of Sarah, Rachel, Hannah, and any of the other infertile women in the Bible reveals some things about what it means to be a person of faith struggling with infertility. A reader who identifies with these women learns that it is absolutely normal to feel the wide range of emotions that an infertile woman feels; these women felt anger, disappointment, frustration, jealousy, and desperation. Any discussion about infertility or care for infertile couples requires giving them permission to feel all of these emotions.

The second thing these women teach the infertile couple is that it is perfectly acceptable to cry out to God. God knows our needs and the desires of our hearts before we open our mouths to pray. If you are experiencing infertility, give yourself permission to pray for a child and express to God the anger and frustration you are feeling. I truly think God would rather hear our desperate and angry cries than for us to be silent and never pray at all. In addition, creating silence in my prayer time to listen for God's direction is helpful in my prayer life. Sometimes in prayer we talk too much! In dealing with infertility, creating silence in your personal prayer time and in your prayer life as a couple can allow you to be more open and receptive to what God is trying to communicate with you.

The third lesson an infertile person can learn from these sisters of the Bible is the notion that children belong to God. However the miracle of parenting enters a couple's life together, the truth is the child belongs to God. A community of faith can be a tremendous support for couples as they go through infertility struggles. Unfortunately, many couples are private about their journeys to become parents. If a faith community can acknowledge that infertility is a tough situation to face alone and that all children belong to God, perhaps the church can do things to be a more supportive community for those facing infertility.

### What the Church Needs to Know about Infertility

I never made an announcement from the pulpit that my husband and I were trying to get pregnant. Just like many other issues involving sexuality, for most couples infertility is a private matter. Church members and pastors need to realize that even if they do not know of anyone with infertility issues, someone in the congregation currently is or has been infertile. Because one in eight couples deal with infertility, it is a very real issue for at least one couple in every congregation. Some couples will never reveal to anyone at church that they are struggling while others will seek out support from church members or pastors. The church needs to acknowledge infertility as a reality in its midst.

Each couple's journey through infertility looks different. A couple is considered infertile if they have been trying for a year to get pregnant without success. Some couples will achieve pregnancy through fertility medication; some will try assisted reproductive technologies such as intrauterine insemination or in vitro fertilization. Many will endure expensive and painful diagnostic tests, and some will be left with the frustrating diagnosis that they have unexplained infertility. I have one friend who swears by the herbal remedy she took that resulted in a pregnancy after years of trying to conceive. Depending on their insurance coverage and their credit limit, some couples will spend all the money they have access to trying to conceive, and their efforts will still not result in a pregnancy. Some couples will endure the emotional pain of fertility treatments and negative pregnancy tests and decide they need to stop.

While couples are trying to conceive, it is helpful if people in the church family can understand the emotional and financial stress that comes from fertility treatments. Fertility treatments are calculated and scientific. I remember having to leave work one day at the drop of a hat and drive two hours to the fertility center, just to be told that I didn't produce a viable egg that month and that we would not be able to do an insemination procedure. Disappointment and heartache exacerbated by the emotional and financial stress of fertility treatments can cause stress at work and at home for infertile couples.

### What the Church Can Do

One of the best ways that the church can minister to infertile couples is by *connecting people who struggle with infertility.* As soon as I felt stressed and overwhelmed by the pressure of infertility treatments, I looked for a tribe of women who shared similar experiences. In her book *Tribal Church:*

*Ministering to the Missing Generation,*[2] author Carol Howard
Merritt talks about the situation of modern young adults. Many
of us do not live near our own families, and we move around
a lot. Our average stay at a job is 2.6 years. All this transition
means we look for communities of support wherever we go.
These people who love and support us, who share their stories
and their lives with us become our tribe.

For me, I needed a tribe of women who understood what it
was like to go through the experience of infertility. I looked for
these women at church, and I approached them carefully and
cautiously. First, I asked a friend who I knew had experienced
infertility struggles, including a conception and miscarriage. I
acknowledged that she might not be ready to talk with me. I
told her that I would love to talk with her about my journey
to get pregnant. So we met for tea and talked, and then kept
meeting monthly. Our tea time is a tremendous support for
me. Another friend became a part of my tribe after a baby
dedication when she looked me in the eye and said, "When
will it be our turn?" She is another safe person to go to talk
about frustrations and disappointments. Another woman in my
tribe has a beautiful son, whom she thanks God for every day.
She and her husband waited ten years to become parents. She
knows what it is like to face the stress of infertility. The more
open I am to talking about my experiences, the more women
join my tribe of support.

Concerned church friends and pastors need to cultivate
sensitivity, remembering that anything someone says to you
about their difficulty becoming pregnant is confidential.
However, with permission obtained from both sides, you might
find opportunities for connections to form between church
members who know the same hardships. The church might
even be willing to open its doors to *hosting an infertility support
group,* like the ones sponsored by Resolve.org. As I looked for a
support group, I found nothing within a hundred miles of my
area. The church could provide a much needed service to the
community by hosting an infertility support group.

As a church we can also *be sensitive about infertility issues
when it comes to worship and other church activities.* Think about
how you would feel to be a couple struggling with infertility

Churches could host
infertility support groups

Mustard Seed-Sized Faith

on Mother's Day or Father's Day at church. If a gift is given in worship to each mother in the congregation, a woman who desires with all her heart to be a mother can feel excluded and miserable. At our church when we present gifts for Mother's or Father's Day, each woman or man at the service that day gets a gift. This past Mother's Day I read a prayer written by Reverend Abi Carlisle-Wilke, a Methodist pastor. She wrote this in a Sunday prayer for the Rev Gal Blog Pals blog ring as part of a Pentecost and Mother's Day prayer:

> Holy one, we also today lift up moms everywhere; we who are moms presently, our moms, moms to be, moms who are now gone on from us, moms whose children have died before them, moms all around the world. We pray for those whose moms weren't able to really parent them, who were abusive, or had mental illnesses, or drug or alcohol abuses, other problems that affected their mothering. We pray for those who are childless not by choice; those who may be trying different medical treatments, or going through the adoption processes, or other means, or those who can't afford it at all. We pray for those who are not mothers by choice; whether by timing, situation, or just by choice, we don't want to leave them out as you don't. Lord we pray for moms whose children have made them happy and those whose children have disappointed them. We pray for those moms in countries that have less than we do trying to make sure their kids have the basics. We pray for those moms in countries who have to figure out how to protect their kids from war, the rebels, the terrorists, and the means of war left behind. And we pray for those moms who have been through the recent natural disasters trying to remake life, provide shelter, and who may also grieve the death of their children.[3]

Carlisle-Wilke mentions all types of mothers in this prayer. The way she includes so many different mothering situations helps the infertile woman feel less isolated on Mother's Day at church. In addition, baby showers and baby dedications can be events too hard to deal with for an infertile couple. Understand if a woman says that she cannot attend or host a shower, or help with a baby dedication. If you are a woman dealing with infertility, do not feel obligated to attend these events if you don't feel like it. I grant you permission to skip out!

Another thing pastors can do is to not be afraid to address infertility. Do not skip over the texts in the Bible that contain the stories of infertile couples. By choosing to preach on one of those stories, pastoral leaders might do wonders for the spiritual lives of couples in their congregations who face infertility. If nothing else, the biblical stories of infertility remind couples that they are not alone, even if they could never bring themselves to ask for support.

> The biblical stories of infertility remind couples that they are not alone.

What if the church became a place where infertile couples felt like they could cry out and be heard? What if they felt like they could ask for prayers for their fertility without feeling awkward? What if each couple who longs for a child could be surrounded by a supportive "tribe" who either was experiencing or had experienced some of the same things they had been through? If these things were true then, I think a church could feel good about being the kind of supportive community God intended for it to be. Infertility is one of the many challenges the people of God face each day, and the church has an opportunity to minister to people in this situation.

The conversations that have been most helpful along our journey are not the ones that have offered advice to my husband and me. I have not enjoyed the stories shared with me about how easy it was for a person to get pregnant or the stories of couples who have quit trying to conceive and then gotten pregnant (stopping treatment is not actually a cure for infertility!). The most helpful conversations with people at my church have been the ones that came from a place of authenticity where someone looked me in the eye and said, "I'm sorry you are struggling; I'm praying for you." Honest, kind words from people who have not experienced infertility and my supportive tribe of women are gifts my church gives me.

The ideas presented here for churches to consider are ideas that I hope my own church will implement. Churches have a unique opportunity to be places of support for young adults who struggle with infertility. With God's help, I pray that we will live into being that supportive community. My own church is a wonderful place where I have gained strength, been prayed for, and shared my story with others. All these things have helped my husband and me to feel less isolated as we continue this infertility journey. We still have that mustard seed–sized faith that it takes to know in our hearts that we will be parents. For churches, my hope is that we begin to open our eyes to the fertility issues that our members face. For those on the journey, I hope you will feel supported by your faith community, even if that means you have to do some educating to help them understand. Mustard seed blessings to all.

### Bibliography

Carlisle-Wilke, Reverend Abi. Prayer can be found at: Revgalblogpals.com, http://revgalblogpals.blogspot.com/2008/05/pentecostmothers-sundays-prayer.html.

Howard Merrit, Carol. *Tribal Church: Ministering to the Missing Generation.* Washington, D.C.: Alban Institute, 2007.

### Additional Resources

Domar, Alice D., and Alice Lesch Kelly. *Conquering Infertility: Dr. Alice Domar's Mind/Body Guide to Enhancing Fertility and Coping with Infertility.* New York: Penguin, 2002.

RESOLVE, the national infertility association, www.Resolve.org.

Saake, Jennifer. *Hannah's Hope: Seeking God's Heart in the Midst of Infertility, Miscarriage, and Adoption Loss.* Colorado Springs: NavPress, 2005.

Shalesky, Marlo. *Empty Womb, Aching Heart: Hope and Help for those Struggling with Infertility.* Bloomington, Minn.: Bethany House, 2001.

# Questions \ for Discussion and Contemplation

**1** Throughout her essay, Ridings retains a sense that God is present in the process of conception, that conceiving is, in some way, a divine miracle. Do you think that God chooses which couples become parents and which do not? Why? Does God have a plan this specific or is this a human issue over which God grieves?

**2** If you attend a church, what rituals or traditions do you participate in that might be an unintentional cause of pain to infertile couples? In what ways could these rituals be reworked to offer support?

**3** In this day and age, it's likely that you or someone you know has experienced infertility. Can you share this experience? What does the journey look like from your perspective? Using Ridings' suggestions, how can each person be more concretely supportive to infertile couples they may know?

wtf?

# Notes

## Chapter 1: The Silver Ring and the Ring of Fire

[1]"FAQ About TLW for Youth," http://www.lifeway.com/tlw/faq/, accessed September 15, 2009.

## Chapter 2: Hookup Jesus

[1]Laura Sessions Stepp, *Unhooked: How Young Women Pursue Sex, Delay Love, and Lose at Both* (New York: Riverhead, 2007).

[2]Michael Kimmel, *Guyland: The Perilous World Where Boys Become Men* (New York: HarperCollins, 2008).

[3]Stepp, *Unhooked*, 36.

[4]Ibid., 202.

[5]Unlike the large universities Stepp visited, my college did indeed have single-sex dorms with regulated visitation hours. However, they were hardly ever enforced and easily ignored.

[6]Donna Freitas, *Sex and the Soul: Juggling Sexuality, Spirituality, Romance, and Religion on America's College Campuses* (New York: Oxford, 2008).

[7]Ibid., 194.

[8]Ibid., 200.

[9]Ibid., 152.

[10]Ibid., 217.

[11]Ibid.

[12]Ibid., 239.

## Chapter 3: Sexuality Education in the Church

[1]Sexually Transmitted Infections: many people still refer to these as STDs or Sexually Transmitted Diseases. The leadership at CLER Ministries prefers the use of the term *STI*.

[2]The Southwest Region of the Christian Church (Disciples of Christ) is divided into areas. The Central Area, which includes Midland, Texas, is where the first CLER Ministries camp took place.

[3]CYF—This stands for "Christian Youth Fellowship" and is the typical designation for high-school-aged youth groups in Disciples Churches.

[4]In the early years of Eighters' Camp, Linda and Richard Goddard were the sole keynoting team. As CLER Ministries has grown and spread to new regions of the country, new keynoting teams have been selected and trained. Every CLER Ministries camp has a pair of keynoters consisting of a woman and a man who share the keynote, workshop, and storytelling duties for the week.

## Chapter 4: Christianity

[1]Sallie McFague, *The Body of God: An Ecological Theology* (Minneapolis: Fortress Press, 1993), 16.

[2]Ibid., 23.

[3]Ibid., 109

## Chapter 5: Growing Up Gay

[1]Chris Glaser, *Uncommon Calling: A Gay Christian's Struggle to Serve the Church* (Louisville: Westminster / John Knox Press, 1988), 23–24.

[2]Christine E. Gudorf, *Body, Sex, and Pleasure: Reconstructing Christian Sexual Ethics* (Cleveland: The Pilgrim Press, 1994), 83.

[3]Ibid., 30.

## Chapter 6: Porn Nation

[1]Will McBride, *Show Me! A Picture Book of Sex for Children and Parents* (New York; St. Martins Press, 1975).

[2]Margaret R. Miles, "God's Love, Mother's Milk," *Christian Century* (January 29, 2008).

## Chapter 8: In Vitro Fertilization

[1]Fertility Associates of Memphis, "2007 Success Rates for Assisted Reproductive Techniques," http://www.fertilitymemphis.com/documents/2007_IVF_Success_Rate_Handout.pdf.

## Chapter 9: "A Wild Ass at Home in the Wilderness"

[1]Kind of makes you picture doing it with a fork, doesn't it? Though the evidence is contested, I think the choice of this word lends credibility to those who suggest Shakespeare helped write the KJV.

[2]Eugene Peterson, *The Message: Remix* (Colorado Springs: NavPress, 2003). Though some of my academic pals sniff at the *Message* because it's not a literal translation, I think it is immensely helpful for devotional use.

[3]Athanasius, *Ad Antiochenos 5.6-11; Contra Arianos 2.33; 3.1f, 15; Ad Afros II; In illud omnia 5; Expositio fidei 1-4*. Found in Thomas Forsyth Torrance, *Trinitarian Perspectives* (Edinburgh: T&T Clark, 1999), 140.

[4]I read that fact in an article by David Barash on Salon.com, titled "The Myth of Monogamy," http://archive.salon.com/sex/feature/2001/01/23/monogamy/index.html, January 3, 2001. He and his wife, Judith Eve Lipton, wrote a book by the same title (New York: W. H. Freeman and Co., 2001).

[5]Rob Bell, *Nooma 02: Flame* (video) (Grand Rapids: Zondervan, 2007).

[6]Eugene Peterson quite accurately calls these three *mys* the "Replacement Trinity" in *Eat This Book* (Grand Rapids: Eerdmans, 2006), 31–35.

[7]These mystical poets are collected with eight others from around the world with Daniel Ladinsky's bold and fresh translation in *Love Poems from God: Twelve Sacred Voices from the East and West* (New York: Penguin, 2002).

[8]A great book on this exact topic by someone I count as a friend is Belden Lane's *The Solace of Fierce Landscapes: Exploring Desert and Mountain Spirituality* (New York: Oxford U.P., 1998).

[9]A wonderful ethic for life and relationship is articulated in Rabbi Martin Buber's classic *I and Thou*, originally published in German in 1923, and still available in English from several publishers.

[10]Yes, it's true! Fully customizable, interactive, sex slave robot mannequins are on the market. Vince Neil is an enthusiast of the $15,000 Realdoll "companions," and Howard Stern has given his personal recommendation after an on-air "test" of the product. The patented Face-X technology even allows you to switch out the face on your doll's body.

[11]Amy Frykholm, "Addicted: Pastors and Pornography," *The Christian Century* (September 4, 2007).

[12]Gretel Kovach, "Pastor's Advice for a Better Marriage: More Sex," *The New York Times*, November 24, 2008. Newspaper online available from http://www.nytimes.com/2008/11/24/us/24sex.html?hp, accessed September 15, 2009.

[13]In cases where Christianity has been co-opted by the culture, that bastardized form of the faith has also been used for the promotion of such things.

## Chapter 10: Mustard Seed-Sized Faith

[1]I took two fertility drugs, Femara and Clomid, in hopes of stimulating my ovaries to ovulate.

[2]Carol Howard Merritt, *Tribal Church: Ministering to the Missing Generation* (Washington, D.C.: The Alban Institute, 2007).

[3]Permission to use blog entry given by Rev. Abi Carlisle-Wilke.

Notes

131

# Volume Contributors

**Mary Allison Beasley Cates** was ordained in the Presbyterian Church (U.S.A) after earning her B.A. in Religious Studies at Rhodes College and M. Div. at Vanderbilt Divinity School. She currently resides in Memphis, Tennessee, with her husband and toddler son and serves as a part-time parish associate at Shady Grove Presbyterian Church. After another successful IVF, Mary Allison gave birth to a baby boy in January of 2009.

**Jackson Culpepper** survived True Love Waits, Judgment Houses, and WWJD bracelets to go on and write fiction, poetry, and this essay. He is currently in the Master of Fine Arts (MFA) program at the University of South Carolina. He likes fishing, bluegrass, and old black-and-white samurai movies.

**Heather Godsey** is an ordained minister of the Christian Church (Disciples of Christ) currently serving as the program director for the Wesley Foundation at the University of Tennessee. She lives in Knoxville with her husband and two dogs who insist on helping her write.

**Nathan Mattox** is an ordained elder in the United Methodist Church who currently serves a church in Morris, Oklahoma. He has had the opportunity to live out his calling to ministry in a college setting, as well at UCLA and Occidental College. He lives with an adventurous boy, a darling girl, a beautiful woman, and a cat named Lao-Tzu. His blog on theology, arts, trees, childhood, and culture, *Leaves from the Notebook of a Tamed Optimist,* can be found at www.nathanmattox.blogspot.com.

**L. Shannon Moore** is a freelance writer, musician, and unordained minister. He holds a Bachelor's Degree in Music from East Carolina University and the Master of Divinity from Brite Divinity School, Texas Christian University. He is the Minister of Music and Worship at Central Christian Church in Weatherford, Texas, and lives in Fort Worth.

**Christian Piatt** is an author, speaker, and musician, and serves as coeditor of the WTF? (Where's the Faith?) book series. He cofounded Milagro Christian Church with his wife, Amy, in Pueblo, Colorado, where he serves as worship leader and music minister. He and Amy coauthored *MySpace to Sacred Space: God for a New Generation* (Chalice Press).

**Lara Blackwood Pickrel** is an ordained minister of the Christian Church (Disciples of Christ) and currently serves as minister for youth and young adults at Hillside Christian Church in Kansas City, Missouri. She considers the following things crucial to her character: a passionate love for black jellybeans, words, books, and eloquent turns of phrase; her husband, Chuck Pickrel (who keeps her roots watered whenever she soars); and soul-friends who are companions on the journey.

**Sunny Buchanan Ridings** is the associate minister at First Christian Church in Livingston, Tennessee. She has been happily serving in Livingston since she graduated from Vanderbilt Divinity School in May 2004. She lives with her husband, David, dog, Dolly, and cat, Willie. The Ridings hope to expand their family through birth or adoption soon.

**Sarah Trotter Stewart** lives in Wichita Falls, Texas, with her husband, Karl, and her son, Michael. She holds a bachelors degree in English and a masters degree in English both from Midwestern State University. She continues to counsel Eighters' Camps for the Central Area of the Southwest Region of the Christian Church (Disciples of Christ).

**Shelli R. Yoder,** M.S., M.Div., has worked in the field of body image, eating disorders, nutrition, fitness, and weight concerns for over fifteen years. She is the executive director of the Eating Disorders Coalition of Tennessee and an active member in the United Church of Christ. She resides in Bloomington, Indiana, with her husband and three children.

# From Twilight to Breaking Dawn
*Religious Themes in the Twilight Saga*

By Sandra L. Gravett

Stephenie Meyer's *Twilight* books took the young adult fiction world by storm—topping the bestsellers list with all four titles. The movies that have followed have been equally popular, breaking box office records. The story of a young woman, Bella Swan, and her love affair with the eternally seventeen-year-old vampire Edward Cullen further prompted an entire cottage industry of products, Web sites, and parties, and even resulted in record sales of clothing items worn in the movie.

These books have introduced a variety of topics from young love, to abstinence, to the value of family and friends. But the author, a devout Mormon, also infuses her stories with religious themes and images.

Sandra Gravett examines this intersection between religious themes and the novels/movies. She dissects the relationship between free will and determinism and the importance of choice threads thematically through all four volumes. Love as an agent of change and a motivational impulse for self-sacrifice receives significant emphasis. Images of the garden and the peaceable kingdom provide frames for the story.

Beginning with a short synopsis of each narrative to situate the reader, Gravett proceeds in separate chapters to explore the two major characters, Bella and Edward, with a focus on the use of Eve and Mary as patterns for Bella and of Edward as a Christ-figure.

978-08272-10479, $14.99

CPSIA information can be obtained
at www.ICGtesting.com
Printed in the USA
FFOW04n0115130116
20362FF